T0302458

Transforming Global Education Through Evidence

An Evaluation System for the BHP Foundation's Education Equity Global Signature Program

BENJAMIN K. MASTER, SHELLY CULBERTSON, BRIAN PHILLIPS, ELAINE LIN WANG, HAROLD D. GREEN, JOE FRANCOMBE, HAMISH EVANS, SUSAN GUTHRIE

Sponsored by the BHP Foundation

RAND EDUCATION AND LABOR

For more information on this publication, visit www.rand.org/t/RRA239-1

Library of Congress Cataloging-in-Publication Data is available for this publication.
ISBN: 978-1-9774-0680-4

Published by the RAND Corporation, Santa Monica, Calif.

Cover image composite design: Rick Penn-Kraus, asus/Getty Images

Preface

The BHP Foundation is investing significantly in global education programs and initiatives that are intended to improve the use of evidence to enhance education and learning. In this report, we present a system to evaluate this investment during a five-year period. We provide a strategic theory of change, an analysis of challenges and lessons learned through the initiative to date, a framework of indicators to measure progress, an approach to analyze networks in support of better use of evidence in education, and a comparison with other similar foundations or social investment initiatives. Our system offers an evaluation framework for a philanthropic education program, an approach to understanding this program's contribution and place in the broader global education reform movement, and a case study of how this program conceptualizes and measures its own progress. This report will be of interest to the BHP Foundation and its program partners, policymakers engaged in global education, other foundations interested in evaluation models, and academics.

This study was undertaken by RAND Education and Labor, a division of the RAND Corporation that conducts research on early childhood through postsecondary education programs, workforce development, and programs and policies affecting workers, entrepreneurship, and financial literacy and decisionmaking. This study was sponsored by the BHP Foundation. The BHP Foundation is committed to improving educational equity for underserved students around the world.

More information about RAND can be found at www.rand.org. Questions about this report should be directed to Benjamin Master (bmaster@rand.org), and questions about RAND Education and Labor should be directed to educationandlabor@rand.org.

Contents

Figures

Tables

Summary

There is a critical need to improve education around the globe. Millions of children and youth worldwide either do not access educational opportunities or receive an education of insufficient quality to provide them the tools needed to thrive, leaving them unable to participate to the fullest in the economy. Recognition of these deficits has led governments and international organizations to make significant investments in education, but huge gaps remain.

The BHP Foundation has prioritized investing in global education. The BHP Foundation conducted an analysis of gaps in the global education landscape to determine the focus of its education investments. This process included studying the findings of major global education reports and hosting an Education Equity Workshop in Melbourne in 2016 to discuss gaps that could be filled; attendees included representatives of leading international institutions, industry bodies, and civil society organizations. After this consultative process, the BHP Foundation identified a key challenge: Much evidence exists about how to improve education, but these findings often are not implemented. To address this deficit, the BHP Foundation created the Education Equity Global Signature Program (hereafter referred to as the Program) in 2017 (projects were first funded in 2018). Through the Program, the BHP Foundation aims to make investments that help translate evidence about improving education into practice. To achieve its ambitious goals, the Program is funding five partner organizations that seek to translate research findings into global education practice: the Education Endowment Foundation, UN Women, the Brookings Institution, Teach for All, and the Global Business Coalition for Education. Four of these organizations began their BHP Foundation–funded work in 2018, with the fifth starting in 2020.

As a new and smaller actor in global education, the BHP Foundation aims to make investments that contribute to step changes in improving education in low- and middle-income countries and improving education in disadvantaged communities in high-income countries. Program leadership views a *step change* as a significant, measurable improvement in some aspect of education that is greater than incremental improvement. Specifically, the Program is driven by the theory that such improvements can be brought about by the introduction of evidence about how to do something more effectively, reliance by decisionmakers on evidence, or implementation of evidence-based practice—for example, delivering services or engaging stakeholders. To this end, the Program is investing in activities that seek to connect the education evidence base with educational practice; in particular, the Program aims to enhance opportunities for the education sector to measure performance and impact, help education leaders use evidence to inform decisionmaking, support evidence-based innovation to disrupt current trends in the disparity of education outcomes, and harness the power and influence of education thought leaders to influence public policy.

In support of these goals, the RAND Corporation is conducting a five-year evaluation of the Program. Our evaluation will assess the effectiveness of the Program's strategy and its collective investment in the activities of its partners. This report is the first in a series of three planned reports in which RAND will share its findings. This report summarizes the evaluation system that we developed for this effort and presents initial findings. The components of the evaluation system are the following:

- **Theory of change:** We worked collaboratively with the BHP Foundation to articulate the goals, assumptions, and mechanisms needed to carry out its strategy.
- **Indicator framework:** We identified key indicators that we will use to evaluate impact over the next several years, drawing from partners' own indicators.
- **Qualitative analysis of partner activities, challenges, and lessons learned:** We are conducting interviews with partners and reviewing their documents to understand how the activities of the partners contribute to the Program's impacts.
- **Network analysis:** We are conducting network analyses to understand how different types of networks can be used to translate evidence into educational practice through, for example, policy change, norm spreading, and program implementation.
- **Comparison with other foundations and social investment initiatives:** We conducted interviews and reviewed documents related to six other major funders or implementers of social change initiatives to understand how the BHP Foundation's strategy compares with and contributes to the broader landscape of global educational investments.

In this early stage of evaluation, our findings regarding the progress and impacts of the Program are limited. Each of the partner programs is midstream in its funded work; therefore, many anticipated milestones have yet to be reached. We have gathered perspectives and documentation from leaders managing the work of the BHP Foundation's partners; we expect that in future reports we will be able to delve into specific details of their efforts and analyze their progress over time. In the longer term, our research will depend primarily on data gathered through individual partners' own evaluation efforts. Therefore, our findings will be influenced by the rigor and foci of those evaluations.

In this report, we primarily focus on the Program's strategy, our planned evaluation framework, and a comparative analysis of the BHP Foundation's approach relative to comparator organizations that are engaged in similar efforts. We hope that our evaluation methods for the Program will provide a model for other evaluations of similar efforts, and that our three-report series will ultimately serve as a useful case study of the evolution of a major new philanthropic program's strategy over time.

Acknowledgments

This report relied on information gathered in the first year of a multiyear evaluation of the BHP Foundation's Education Equity Global Signature Program. We are grateful to the project leads of each of the five BHP Foundation–funded partners for speaking with us about their efforts to improve education around the world through prioritizing the use of evidence. The report would not have been possible without their willing participation in all our data collection activities.

We are grateful to the BHP Foundation for supporting the evaluation and this report. We especially thank Brodie Vansleve, the program director for Global Education and North America for the BHP Foundation, and Executive Officer and President of the BHP Foundation James Ensor for their guidance.

We greatly appreciate the feedback provided by our peer reviewers, Julie Bélanger and Julia Kaufman. Their critical insights led to an improved product.

Several RAND staff members supported the publishing of this report. In addition to the authors, Jenna Kramer contributed to the literature review. Fatih Unlu provided insightful feedback on drafts of the report during the quality assurance process, Kristin Leuschner assisted with communications analysis, and Kristen Meadows formatted key graphics. We also thank Jessica Wolpert for a careful copyedit. The authors take full responsibility for any errors in the report.

Abbreviations

Alliance	Alliance for Useful Evidence
COVID-19	coronavirus disease 2019
CUE	Center for Universal Education at the Brookings Institution
EDC	Education Development Center
EDCTP	European and Developing Countries Clinical Trials Partnership
EEF	Education Endowment Foundation
Gates Foundation	Bill & Melinda Gates Foundation
GBC-Ed	Global Business Coalition for Education
J-PAL	Abdul Latif Jameel Poverty Action Lab
OECD	Organisation for Economic Co-operation and Development
Program	Education Equity Global Signature Program
RCT	randomized controlled trial
SABER	Systems Approach for Better Education Results
SDG	Sustainable Development Goal
SMART	specific, measurable, appropriate, reliable, and time-bound
TaRL	Teaching at the Right Level
TFA	Teach for All
UNESCO	United Nations Educational, Scientific and Cultural Organization
UNW	UN Women

CHAPTER ONE

Introduction

In a global economy that increasingly rewards highly skilled workers, low- and middle-income countries face the challenge of adequately educating their children and youth. Hundreds of millions of youth worldwide are deficient in the basic skills needed to support themselves and their families and to participate as citizens, affecting the future of economic and social development in their countries. In low- and middle-income countries, more than half of children are not minimally proficient in reading by the end of primary school; this rate is 90 percent in low-income countries (World Bank, 2019a). Meanwhile, rates of secondary school enrollment have plateaued; 40 percent of lower secondary school-age and 60 percent of upper secondary school-age children in low-income countries are not in school (United Nations Educational, Scientific and Cultural Organization [UNESCO], Institute for Statistics, 2019). In addition, only half of countries with data have similar primary and secondary educational outcomes for girls and boys (UNESCO, 2016b).

A complex and varied set of interacting factors have led to this global learning crisis. These include the following (Pritchett, Woolcock, and Andrews, 2010; UNESCO, 2020; World Bank, 2018a and 2018b): poverty, weak institutions that fail to keep up with needs of growing populations, the legacy of colonialism, poor alignment between the activities of development actors and governments, "state capability traps" in which the state's limited administrative capability to implement policies and programs limits what can be achieved, lack of institutions or misalignment of institutions with learning, competing priorities of multiple stakeholders, gender norms, lack of infrastructure, poor curricula, policies that are not followed, and untargeted finance.

In recognition of the importance of education and the deficits in education in many settings, the BHP Foundation has decided to make global education a priority for its philanthropic investments. The BHP Foundation conducted an analysis of gaps in the global education landscape to determine the focus of its education investments and how the BHP Foundation could most effectively contribute. This process included studying the findings of major global education reports and hosting the Education Equity Workshop in Melbourne in 2016 with representatives of leading international institutions, industry bodies, and civil society organizations to discuss gaps that could be filled and where other philanthropic actors were less engaged. The BHP Foundation then made a decision to align its strategy with analysis stemming from pivotal global education reports.

Two recent reports particularly informed the BHP Foundation's view that this crisis is linked both to inadequate investments in education and to challenges in prioritizing the most efficient and effective policies, interventions, and investment opportunities. In its 2016 *Learning Generation* report, the Education Commission called for the governments of developing countries and the international community to increase funding for education. It also called for sustained efforts to strengthen education systems based on evidence to enhance confidence that investments are making a difference. The Education Commission called for focusing on performance, exploring innovative approaches, targeting the most vulnerable, and marshaling the collective resources of education stakeholders around the world to address key inequities in education within a generation (Education Commission, International Commission on Financing Global Education Opportunity, 2016). A subsequent report by the Education Commission et al. (2018) highlighted the importance of building out knowledge-sharing infrastructure, including by pairing research, data, and tools with capacity development and fostering networks to facilitate the transfer of evidence to practice.

An insight that BHP Foundation leadership took from the consultative process and global reports was that if "business as usual" continued in global education, incremental change and improvement would still occur. However, the scale of the challenge, combined with population growth, means that educational outcomes could be worse for greater numbers of people in 2030 if current trends continue. As a new actor in the field, the BHP Foundation believed that it had the luxuries of investing in underinvested areas and taking risks by investing in big ideas.

With this challenge in mind, in 2017, the BHP Foundation launched its Education Equity Global Signature Program (hereafter referred to as the Program), which offered an ambitious vision for improving education globally: "to enhance opportunities for disadvantaged young people to access, participate in and achieve a quality education and, through this, strengthen the civil and economic components of society."[1]

As a new and smaller actor in global education, the BHP Foundation aims to make investments that contribute step changes in improving education in both low- and middle-income countries and improving education in disadvantaged communities in high-income countries. Program leadership views a *step change* as a significant, measurable improvement in some aspect of education that is greater than incremental improvement. Specifically, the Program is driven by the theory that such improvements can be brought about by the introduction of evidence about how to do something more effectively, reliance by decisionmakers on evidence, or implementation of evidence-based practice—for example, delivering services or engaging stakeholders.

---

[1] In 2015, the BHP Foundation established three global priority program areas: Education Equity, Natural Resource Governance, and Environmental Resilience.

To this end, the Program is investing in activities that seek to connect the education evidence base with educational practice; in particular, the Program aims to enhance opportunities for the education sector to measure performance and impact, help education leaders use evidence to inform decisionmaking, support evidence-based innovation to disrupt current trends in the disparity of education outcomes, and harness the power and influence of education thought leaders to influence public policy. The Program is aiming for step changes because of concern that the "business as usual" approach in global education means that current educational trends that leave out too many would otherwise continue. Its efforts support the following four aims:

1. Enhance opportunities for the education sector to measure performance and impact.
2. Enhance opportunities for education leaders to use evidence to inform decisionmaking.
3. Support evidence-based innovation to disrupt current trends in the disparity of education outcomes.
4. Harness the power and influence of education thought leaders to influence public policy through contributing evidence-based data and experience.

To achieve its ambitious goals related to increasing the scale and efficiency of educational investments globally, the BHP Foundation is funding five partners that are addressing these issues in global education: the Education Endowment Foundation (EEF), UN Women (UNW), the Center for Universal Education at the Brookings Institution (CUE), Teach for All (TFA), and the Global Business Coalition for Education (GBC-Ed). The BHP Foundation's first funded projects started in 2018.

In support of the BHP Foundation's goals, the RAND Corporation is conducting a five-year evaluation of the Program. The aims of the evaluation are the following:

1. Contribute to the development and evolution of the Program's strategy by articulating a theory of change.
2. Assess the impacts of the Program across funded partnerships and inform learning and continuous improvement for both the BHP Foundation and its partners.
3. Share lessons learned with the global education community about the results of a social investment initiative that aims to translate evidence into practice.
4. Develop a model for evaluating a foundation's portfolio of investments.

Our evaluation will result in three public reports. This initial report describes a framework to evaluate the Program, explains our methods for assessing progress over the five-year period, and presents some preliminary results after the first year of the evaluation. Our second report will describe progress by year three and provide some midcourse recommendations. Our third and final report will provide a summative assessment of the effectiveness to date of the BHP Foundation's approach for investing in the use of evidence to improve education globally.

How the BHP Foundation's Program Fits into the Global Landscape for International Investment in Education

Governments, multilaterals, and private and nongovernmental organizations have made considerable investments in improving education globally. However, education quality and attainment in many countries still lags behind desired outcomes. The BHP Foundation has selected its investments based on the hypothesis that improving evidence use will speed up advances in education.

The underlying logic of educational investment—education supports democratic societies and knowledge-based economies (Hanushek and Kimko, 2000; Krueger and Lindahl, 2000)—has spurred a worldwide movement focused on investing in improving education quality, access, and inclusiveness. This movement's premise is that the international exchange of education policies and practices, combined with public and private investment, will facilitate education system improvement. This global education reform movement (as defined in Sahlberg, 2006) is a loose coalition of leaders pursuing a global education agenda, which is supported by national and international private and government investments. Investors include national governments and their education ministries or agencies supported by multilateral agencies; nongovernmental organizations; and local, national, and international foundations. Some significant global education initiatives in recent decades have been the United Nations' Millennial Development Goals, which were updated to become the current UN Sustainable Development Goals (SDGs). The SDGs, which were adopted by all UN member states in 2015, provide an influential guiding framework for education initiatives and funding priorities around the world, laying out global goals through 2030. The fourth SDG (hereafter referred to as SDG4) aims to "ensure inclusive and equitable quality education and promote lifelong learning opportunities for all" (UNESCO, 2016a).

Multiple actors have made substantial investments in support of improving education globally. Governments spend an average of 4.8 percent of gross domestic product on the education of their citizens or roughly $4 trillion annually (UNESCO, 2018). Government spending on education is supplemented by public and private investment by multilateral agencies; nongovernmental organizations; and local, national, and international foundations that aim to increase educational access, quality, and equity. Multilateral agencies investing in global education include the United Nations International Children's Emergency Fund (UNICEF), UNESCO, the World Bank, and the Organisation for Economic Co-operation and Development (OECD), among many others. However, current levels of investment are not sufficient to meet commonly held access and equity goals or labor market needs: There is a funding gap between what is needed and what is currently being invested by public and private sources (Winthrop et al., 2013). In addition, funding provided is not always spent effectively and does not necessarily translate into greater educational attainment. Among most OECD countries, for example, higher expenditures on education do not seem to predict student performance, as measured by the OECD Programme for International Student Assessment (OECD, 2020b).

It is in this context that the Program seeks to invest in a range of efforts that support curating the evidence base about how to improve education and implement good practice, with the aim of making global education investment funding more effective.

Our Approach to This Evaluation

We are evaluating the effectiveness of the Program's strategy and its investment in the collective activities of the partners. We note that the BHP Foundation's support for each of its partners includes separate partner-specific evaluations of their own impacts. Our goal is to not duplicate the individual evaluations of each partner's work but to assess the effectiveness of this body of work as a whole.

This evaluation is both formative and summative. The formative component includes articulating the theory of change, helping the BHP Foundation and its partners better understand key pathways to impact, and supporting continuous improvement over the course of the evaluation. By specifying the theory of change and illustrating how this theory has played out in different contexts, the evaluation will illustrate—and test the soundness of—the BHP Foundation's assumptions of how to achieve impact. The summative component will provide our assessment of the Program's overall effectiveness at the end of the evaluation.

Articulating the assumptions underlying this work and determining how these assumptions ultimately play out can support continuous improvement in both the individual partners' work and the evolution of the BHP Foundation's strategy. Findings from our evaluation can also inform the global education field more broadly, particularly the work of other global funders engaged in related efforts.

Furthermore, the BHP Foundation is contributing to common goals in global education supported by many actors around the world. Given this, we will rely on the concept of contribution analysis (Mayne, 2008) during the evaluation. Contribution analysis is "a form of theory-based evaluation where effectiveness is the main question and where experimental designs are not possible" (Wimbush, Montague, and Mulherin, 2012, p. 311). It allows researchers to assess the contribution a program is making to a desired goal, in cases in which it may not be possible to attribute all results to the activities of a single actor. It is a common evaluation approach and has been used in multiple sectors, including in educational contexts.

In this first public report, we describe the evaluation system for understanding the impact of the Program's education efforts and present initial findings in the early stages of the initiative. This evaluation system consists of several components. We list the components here and describe our general approach to evaluation, which will be detailed in the following chapters:

- **Theory of change:** The first component is to describe the Program's theory of change. We worked collaboratively with the BHP Foundation to explicitly articulate the key components of its Program logic model.
- **Indicator framework:** We will make summative measurements of Program-level progress relative to the theory of change, through assessing key indicators. Indicator analysis will track progress of a set of SMART (specific, measurable, appropriate, reliable, and timely) indicators aligned with the Program's theory of change (Doran, 1981).
- **Qualitative analysis of partner activities, challenges, and lessons learned:** We share our plans and some preliminary findings illustrating how the activities of each partner contribute to the Program's impacts. This component of the evaluation will describe key successes and challenges associated with the partners' work, as well as circumstances that facilitate their work toward improving education globally.
- **Network analysis:** Networks are an important area of investment in the Program, according to the hypothesis that translating evidence into practice in education relies on dissemination of information among stakeholders and collaborations of networks of people working toward common goals. In this first report, we illustrate several types of networks through a case study of UNW's networks for policy change, norm spreading, and program implementation.
- **Comparison with other foundations and social investment initiatives:** We also share the results of case studies we conducted of six other organizations engaged in similar work that can serve as a reference point for how the BHP Foundation's strategy compares with and contributes to the broader landscape of global educational investments.

Limitations of Our Evaluation Approach

By design, our evaluation of the BHP Foundation's Program relies heavily on insights from the funded partners and from the evaluations that the BHP Foundation required each of them to conduct as a portion of their funded work. Therefore, the quality of many of the key indicators that we will use to inform our judgment about areas of relative success or challenge for the Program are outside our control. Moreover, our own primary data collection, including interviews, collection of documents, and collection of data on partner networks, is largely descriptive and exploratory in nature and is not designed to infer causation of Program efforts. Our scope does not include independent investigation of the partner activities or staff beyond those we were connected with by the partners directly. (We note that each partner has a separate parallel independent individual evaluation.) Overall, rather than adding substantial new data through our evaluation, our primary focus is on analysis of existing data to better interpret partner-specific evidence in light of the overall Program strategy and objectives.

Road Map of the Report

This report is composed of seven chapters that include both preliminary findings and descriptions of our framework and planned evaluation components for the years ahead. Chapter Two describes the BHP Foundation's theory of change and the partners in which it invests. Chapter Three describes how we will evaluate the Program's success in meeting its goals over this five-year period, with a detailed discussion of our planned indicator framework, the key measures we will track, and the questions we hope to answer through this work. Chapter Four summarizes the primary activities, challenges, and lessons learned to date from the individual efforts of the funded partners. Chapter Five describes how we intend to use network analyses to provide additional formative and summative insights and shares one network analysis case study conducted in the first year of the study. Chapter Six reviews six other education or social investment initiatives and offers lessons learned on good practice in strategy and management as a reference point for the BHP Foundation's strategy. Finally, Chapter Seven summarizes our conclusions and observations to date and looks ahead to future steps in the evaluation of this Program. The appendixes contain more information about indicators, interviews, and network analyses.

CHAPTER TWO

The Program Strategy and Funded Partners

The BHP Foundation's Strategic Vision

The BHP Foundation's leadership, drawing on extensive engagement with global leaders, believes that as a small new actor, the foundation can play a role in contributing to achieving education equity globally by improving the effectiveness of investment and learning outcomes through greater use of evidence to inform decisionmaking. Education is a slow-moving system, often characterized by the continuation of the same approaches that do not produce desired results or by incremental, rather than transformative, changes. According to the views of the BHP Foundation's leadership, if the business-as-usual approach to education—and the amount and types of investment in education—continues, it cannot be reasonably expected that more students will be educated or that students will be better educated and in a strong position to enter the 21st-century workforce.

Bold improvements are needed, and, according to the BHP Foundation's strategic vision, this begins with generating, curating, providing, and disseminating cutting-edge, evidence-backed information for and to stakeholders and decisionmakers. Fundamentally, the idea is to leverage and build upon available evidence about what works to engage and support traditionally disadvantaged learners and close opportunity gaps. The Program therefore focuses on expanding the use of these approaches and understanding how to apply them effectively in various contexts. The BHP Foundation's leadership believes that investing in initiatives that could affect the effectiveness of the system and contribute to a step change will result in an inflection point in the trajectory of securing educational opportunities for all.

The intended beneficiaries of the BHP Foundation initiative are both students in traditional education settings, for whom academic achievement or degree attainment is the main goal, and marginalized or underrepresented learners, such as those outside the formal education system. For some of these marginalized learners, simply accessing educational opportunities can be a challenge.

Articulating the Education Equity Global Signature Program's Theory of Change

To frame our evaluation of the Program strategy and develop the Program-level theory of change (as shown in Figure 2.1), we reviewed both the BHP Foundation's strategy and the plans and logic models of each of the funded partners.

This framework is intended to capture the chief components of the work of the Program's partners and describe how their activities and interim outcomes are expected to contribute to the long-term outcomes and impact that the BHP Foundation hopes to achieve. Although no single partner is engaged in all the activities and interim outcomes described in Figure 2.1, partners' work and interim outcomes collectively constitute the investment that the BHP Foundation has made to achieve its desired impacts.

As illustrated in the figure, collectively Program partners are engaged in multiple activities that focus on improving use of evidence in education: curating evidence about improving education, disseminating evidence-based strategies, developing capacity to leverage evidence, advocating to develop enabling environments, and testing potentially transformative innovation. As such, the bulk of Program investments are focused on developing public goods, such as evidence dissemination and resources to enhance the capacity of local actors to use evidence, with a focus specifically on underserved countries and communities.

These activities are expected to lead to a set of interim outcomes. These outcomes in general are the result of the abilities of education stakeholders to make better use of evidence. These are increased availability of data and evidence, more-informed decision-making, networks of purposeful collaboration, and empowerment though leaders and local actors. The BHP Foundation leadership regards multiple actors—government, school leadership and teachers, nonprofits, philanthropists, grassroots organizations, parents, and the general community—as important for improving education; each is a part of a learner's education process. The BHP Foundation's leadership believes that a necessary shift is to move from a top-down or centralized model, in which local authorities and educators are told what to do, to one that provides local leaders with evidence-based information and empowers them to make decisions. This belief underlies the BHP Foundation's commitment to facilitating systemic improvements by helping local leaders access evidence and strengthen their body of knowledge about what works to improve educational opportunities.

These activities and interim outcomes can be directly measured by indicators in the early years of the program, as they are a direct result of the work of the BHP Foundation partners. These activities and interim outcomes are expected to lead to longer term outcomes and impacts. The BHP Foundation and its partners do not directly control the long-term outcomes and impact, but rather contribute to and influence them; the long-term outcomes and impacts result from the efforts of the full span of education stakeholders described above.

Long-term outcomes of these efforts are expected to be an increased share of investments by others in evidence-based practices, more and more-efficient educational

Figure 2.1
Education Equity Global Signature Program Theory of Change

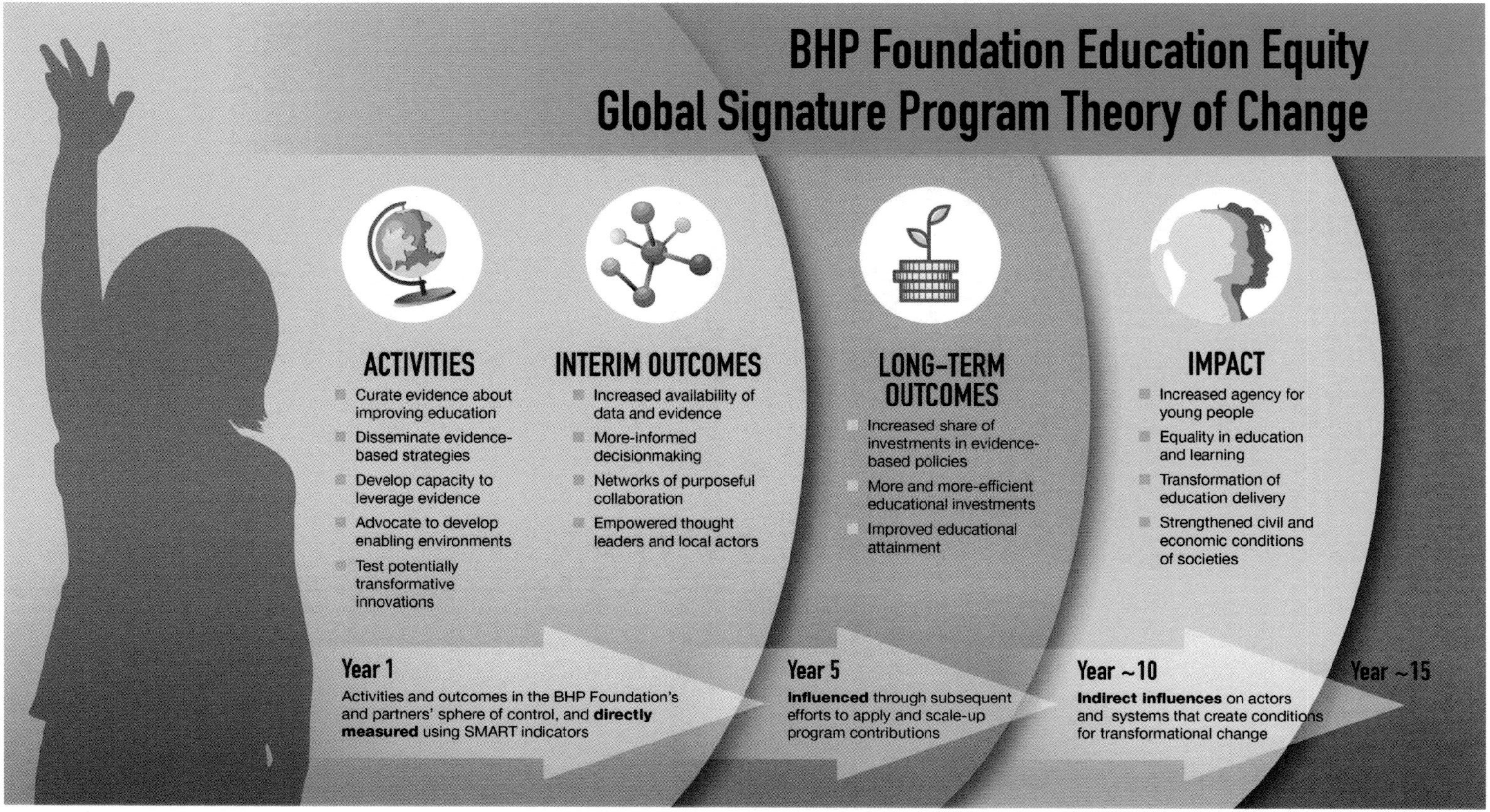

SOURCE: Copyright BHP Foundation; used with permission.

investments, and improved educational attainment in low- and middle-income countries. Knowledge from the prior activities and interim outcomes along the logic model could help others make decisions about and implement processes to better support access to education for underserved populations. Critically, investments should also help create the conditions (e.g., policies, networks) that can scale up and sustain such efforts. Through all this, not only are learners' educational opportunities enhanced, but so is their communities' commitment to helping young people thrive. Local ownership in the effort is essential to ensuring sustainability of change and continued forward movement.

This is a longer-term process—occurring during the next decade—and cannot be measured during the course of this evaluation. Beyond this time period, indicators of the Program's impact include wide adoption and implementation of the evidence-based practices, products, and tools developed by funded partners. This adoption and implementation would be a testament to the usability and applicability of interim outcomes directly resulting from the investment. Another indicator would be an increase in activities aimed at generating new evidence about effective practices, particularly in regions or countries that previously had not prioritized the role of evidence. Eventually, the BHP Foundation hopes that this would lead to consequential change in target learners' skills and capabilities. The BHP Foundation expects that a longer-term outcome of the Program will be change in local, regional, and national policies, dialogues, and action around who needs to be better served by educational services and how barriers can be removed to make that happen. Further into the future, the BHP Foundation hypothesizes that if these steps happen, there will be *impact,* such as increased agency for young people, equality in access to education and learning opportunities, transformation of education delivery, and strengthened civil and economic conditions of societies.

We note that networks play a role in each of the steps along the theory of change; the idea of the creation of a step change relies on networks. BHP Foundation investments often target a specific topic or context, but expanding such improvements from a specific context to a global level will depend on networks. In particular, disseminating evidence, advocating for its use, scaling up evidence, expanding evidence to other contexts, purposeful collaboration, and more depends upon networks of stakeholders and how they interact with each other and the evidence.

As currently drafted, the theory of change shown in Figure 2.1 describes the anticipated sequence of activities and outcomes of the Program, but it does not yet go into detail about the pathways to impact of the individual partners or of the program as a whole. In Chapter Seven, we describe some of our next steps for the evaluation, further unpacking the specific intended pathways to impact of both the Program and partners and more explicitly detailing the assumptions underlying those intended pathways, in support of holistically assessing whether the work ultimately plays out as expected.

About the Partners and Their Contributions to the Program

The BHP Foundation's strategy for the Education Equity Global Signature Program entails investing in a set of mutually reinforcing projects over a five-year period. The five selected projects are managed by five global organizations, each of which brings its existing talent, resources, networks, and experiences to bear on its BHP Foundation–supported work. These five partner organizations each envision certain specific results from the BHP Foundation funding; at the same time, their BHP Foundation–funded workstreams often build upon and contribute to the broader vision and objectives of these organizations. Moreover, the efforts of the individual partner projects may fit in at a different point of the theory of change depicted above for the Program on the whole. In the next section, we briefly summarize the Program's selected partners and projects. We then describe how these five individual projects cohere to contribute to the BHP Foundation's strategy.

Overview of Partners and Projects

The partners are all global organizations, but they vary by type of organization, as well as by size and by the anticipated duration and nature of their BHP Foundation–funded work. Table 2.1 provides a summary of information about the partners and their projects. The projects' BHP Foundation funding varies from about $5 million to about $15 million, with three projects expected to span five years and two expected to span about three years. In several cases, the partners explicitly proposed to pair BHP Foundation funding with outside funding, which is expected to directly support the same streams of their work over the same time span. The partners tend to be headquartered in the United Kingdom or the United States, although their work is international in scope. Figure 2.2 indicates countries where multiple partners are engaged in BHP Foundation–funded work.

The partners' BHP Foundation–funded work encompasses a range of activities collectively designed to further the foundation's objectives. CUE has three principal BHP Foundation–funded workstreams: identifying effective innovations that can rapidly transform education, enhancing the use of data to drive outcomes, and scaling promising innovations. EEF is using BHP Foundation funding to revamp its existing toolkit of research evidence and to partner with organizations around the world to connect research and practice by funding research trials and building out networks of school-based "evidence hubs" to disseminate findings and build capacity. GBC-Ed seeks to foster a global ecosystem of businesses investing in education and to equip business investors with user-friendly tools that facilitate making effective investments. TFA's BHP Foundation–funded work has at its core the expansion of knowledge about what works to effect community-level progress, the use of this knowledge among educators and policymakers, and the development of pipelines of local leaders. UNW is using BHP Foundation funding to pilot its second chance education work to expand

Table 2.1
Overview of Partners and Projects

Partner	Type of Organization and Principal Location	Partner Project Name, Funding, and Duration	Synopsis of Work
CUE	Think tank; United States	• Millions Learning: Evidence and Innovation to Scale Impact • $8.0 million (BHP Foundation), $13.1 million (total) • July 2018–June 2023	• Identify effective innovations to transform education through a global evidence review and country case studies • Develop tools that facilitate decisionmakers' uptake of innovations • Engage with stakeholders to promote use of data to drive outcomes • Implement "Real-Time Scaling Labs" (Robinson, Winthrop, and McGivney, 2016) in several countries to test innovations; share lessons learned; and enhance connections among researchers, practitioners, and policymakers
EEF	Charity; United Kingdom	• Building a Global Evidence Ecosystem for Teaching • £9.9 million • April 2018–March 2023	• Curate, analyze, summarize, and repackage existing research in a form that delivers key actionable insights to teachers and policymakers • Create a fellowship program that contributes to evidence generation and synthesis, as well as mobilization of stakeholders, by drawing in expertise and research from a variety of local contexts • Work with partner organizations across the world to test education interventions, build "evidence hub" networks of schools, and connect research and practice
GBC-Ed	Nonprofit; United Kingdom and United States	• Business Impact for Education Equity • $5.4 million (BHP Foundation), $8.3 million (total) • January 2020–March 2023	• Consolidate and synthesize existing evidence on business investments in education • Incorporate evidence into user-friendly tools that facilitate effective investments • Foster the development of a global ecosystem of businesses and associated stakeholders coordinating to invest strategically in education

Table 2.1—Continued

Partner	Type of Organization and Principal Location	Partner Project Name, Funding, and Duration	Synopsis of Work
TFA	Nonprofit; United Kingdom and United States	• Leadership and Global Impact for Community Learning • $14.8 million (BHP Foundation), $30.0 million (total) • October 2018–September 2023	• Expand knowledge about what works to drive community-level progress and enhance utilization of this knowledge among educators and policymakers • Establish Community Impact Labs as physical and virtual spaces to convene, disseminate findings, and share lessons learned • Build out the Global Learning Lab website to host resources on drivers of progress • Develop pipelines of local leaders and strengthen connections between TFA partner network alumni locally, regionally, and globally
UNW	Multilateral; Switzerland and United States	• Second Chance Education and Vocational Learning Programme • $15.6 million (Phase I of this program) • July 2018–June 2021	• Expand access among marginalized women to high-quality educational content • Connect marginalized women with employment and entrepreneurial activities • Develop and curate content for e-learning platforms, and establish Women's Empowerment Hubs where women can learn and connect with potential employers • Bring together stakeholders from business, government, and the nonprofit community and engage in evidence-based • advocacy to reduce impacts of harmful social norms and foster policy and budgetary changes

Figure 2.2
Countries Where Multiple Partners Are Engaged in BHP Foundation–Funded Project Work

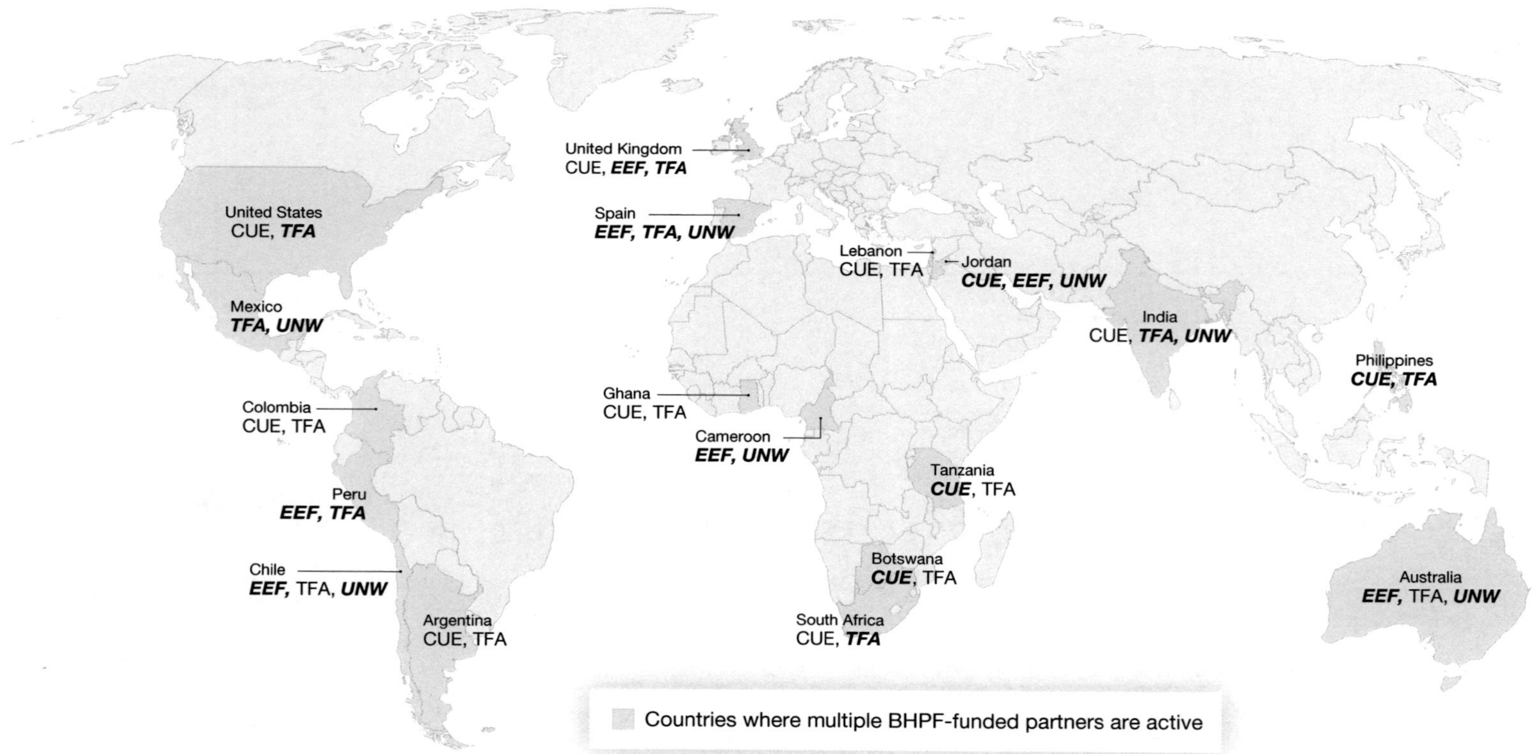

SOURCE: Copyright BHP Foundation; used with permission.
NOTE: ***Bold italic*** text indicates that the partner has significant in-country engagement connected to BHP Foundation–funded work. BHPF = BHP Foundation.

access among marginalized women to high-quality education content, connect women with employment, and engage in advocacy to push for changes to policies and social norms.

Beyond providing funding and supporting each individual partner and project, the BHP Foundation envisions playing multiple other roles in the Program. One critical role is as convener and facilitator of collaboration among funded partners. This involves bringing the partners together and developing a sense of community, so that partners share lessons about their projects for all to learn from; in this respect, there is potential for the Program to be greater than the sum of its parts. Second, the BHP Foundation aims to provide opportunities for the funded partners and other organizations in the greater BHP Foundation orbit to network and benefit from each other's experiences in trying to enact systemic change. The goal is to create forums where organic exchanges of information and leverage points across streams of work can be explored among a group of partners with similar missions but that previously had limited interaction. Finally, aware of its nascency in the area of educational philanthropy, the BHP Foundation positions itself as an inclusive participant and learner in the process. This encompasses several aspects, such as learning more about promising, scalable, evidence-based practices; learning how to best support partners by building their capacity and strengthening their thinking; and, ultimately, learning how to invest for impact in education.

How the Projects Contribute to the BHP Foundation's Strategy

Each of the selected partners and projects contributes to one or more of the activities identified in the theory of change and is responsible for producing interim outcomes that lead to desired long-term outcomes. In Table 2.2, we present a few examples of partner activities for each of the five key activities identified in the theory of change.

We recognize that these examples are not necessarily comprehensive of all the work that any partner may be pursuing in any activity stream.

In line with its belief in the importance of evidence-based approaches, the BHP Foundation sought partners that are leaders in curating and disseminating ideas and approaches that hold promise for producing changes in the educational outcomes of intended beneficiaries at some degree of scale. These are the first two activities listed in the theory of change, and all partners have work planned in these areas. For example, both CUE and EEF will draw upon their prior experience in synthesizing evidence of effective practices and innovations to fill gaps in the current knowledge base. In addition, GBC-Ed aims to develop a best-practice tool to influence business and non-corporate actors to make investments that better contribute to systemic change in the quality of education worldwide.

Beyond assembling and disseminating evidence about what works in education and making it available, multiple partners aim specifically to develop local leaders' and decisionmakers' capacity to leverage the evidence to drive action, the third activity

Table 2.2
Examples of Partner Activities Connected to Theory of Change

Activities Identified in Theory of Change	Examples of Partner Activities
Curate evidence about improving education	• CUE will conduct meta-research on specific topics (e.g., use of educational technology) to identify approaches that support accelerated educational progress. • EEF's existing Teaching and Learning Toolkit summarizes how particular strategies have successfully or unsuccessfully influenced student achievement. EEF will build upon the toolkit in ways that address its applicability for different contexts and target groups. • UNW is building a model for effective second chance education and employment solutions for young and adult women. The evidence produced at global and local levels will be consolidated in a set of second chance education manuals to enable different stakeholders to adapt and scale second chance education solutions in their contexts.
Disseminate evidence-based strategies	• GBC-Ed aims to develop a tool to guide business and noncorporate actors in making investments that contribute to systemic change in the quality of education worldwide. • TFA will generate and publish insights about what differentiates high-performing and fast-improving communities through its Community Impact Lab.
Develop capacity to leverage evidence	• CUE plans to support the capacity of its Scaling Labs partner institutions, training the Scaling Lab managers and staff to design, implement, and report on action research. • CUE will develop capacity to leverage evidence through the creation of a standardized costing tool that is meant to help decisionmakers with the critical cost data needed for resource allocation and program planning. • EEF intends to build the capacity of a network of evidence brokers, providing training to these partner organizations on the use of evidence. • TFA participants and alumni will foster local leaders by drawing on insights generated from the Community Impact Lab about what factors drive change and what effective local leaders do.
Advocate to develop enabling environments	• CUE will support its Scaling Labs in reflecting upon and identifying effective levers within the environment—in particular, political and technical aspects—that contribute to scaling high-quality learning opportunities. • EEF will support evidence brokers in playing an advocacy role in which they champion policy changes that help ensure high-quality learning experiences for all students in their jurisdiction. • EEF will prime the landscape for investing in education by requiring matched funding from philanthropic and government sources for the RCTs it sponsors. • UNW works to raise awareness among local policymakers about the need to educate marginalized women and begin breaking down barriers—including discriminatory social norms and formal policies—that disadvantage this group of learners.
Test potentially transformative innovations	• EEF will fund RCTs designed to test promising approaches in local jurisdictions. • TFA's Community Impact Innovation Fund will test the effectiveness of a community's leadership development practices. • UNW will learn what worked and did not work in its Women's Empowerment Hubs and online learning to support marginalized women to reenter formal education systems or access to paid employment opportunities.

NOTES: The table provides illustrative examples. It is not intended to be a comprehensive inventory of all partner activities as related to each category of activities in the theory of change. RCT = randomized controlled trial.

listed in the theory of change. TFA's project, for example, explicitly focuses on growing leadership capacity within communities and countries worldwide to address issues of inequity in educational opportunities and outcomes. Meanwhile, CUE is supporting the capacity of its Scaling Labs partner institutions (mostly nongovernmental organizations), and EEF is building the capacity of a network of evidence brokers (trusted organizations in each partner country that act as intermediaries between policymakers, academics, and practitioners). As a result of such capacity-building activities, the BHP Foundation's partners aim to contribute to the goals of more-informed decisionmaking and more-empowered local actors.

Partners and projects also fit into the BHP Foundation's overall strategy for the Program by engaging in activities that develop enabling environments for equitable educational opportunities, the fourth activity listed in the theory of change. Many partners are committed to examining the factors—roles, norms, and policies—that facilitate or hinder learners' access to educational opportunities. For instance, CUE's Scaling Labs work to identify contextual factors that contribute to scaling high-quality learning opportunities. Meanwhile, part of EEF's work with its evidence brokers is to support these organizations in playing an advocacy role. Furthermore, UNW is working with local governments and policymakers to raise awareness about the need to educate marginalized women so that they are able to access the formal economy. Altogether, these efforts help ensure that any progress made sustains or continues beyond the BHP Foundation Program.

The final activity depicted in the theory of change concerns testing potentially transformative innovations. Several partners will contribute through this approach. For instance, UNW has established and operates Women's Empowerment Hubs using online learning options with local partners to pilot services to marginalized women in search of continued education or vocational training. EEF's RCTs and TFA's Community Impact Innovation Fund both test promising approaches by having local organizations lead experiments. In all, multiple partners' efforts are intended to generate knowledge about what works to increase learning opportunities and elevate student achievement, particularly across borders.

To carry out these activities and achieve full intended impact, all five partners intend to purposefully develop and use networks. A main type of network is one that supports shared learning. CUE's Scaling Labs, EEF's Evidence Hubs, UNW's Empowerment Hubs, and TFA's Community Impact Labs all exemplify this purpose. These networks are used to convey or test evidence-informed practices and disseminate lessons learned to each other and to the lead organization. A second main type of network is one that mobilizes change, particularly in the broader policy landscape. EEF's network of evidence brokers serves this function. Similarly, TFA aspires to tap into its global network of alumni and staff in partner organizations to enact practices or advocate for conditions that support community progress. UNW aims to develop allies in local governments to facilitate policy discussions and in the private sector to help ensure that the skills and content in its Second Chance Education Programme align with future employment opportunities. Meanwhile, GBC-Ed aims to create a network of effective education investors; if successful, this network can potentially influence the normative practices of the sector.

Collectively, the selected partners also overlap with respect to geographical focus and their specialization with respect to targeted decisionmakers and learners. These areas could lead to informal collaboration and learning opportunities among various partners or synergies that amplify the impact. With respect to geography, for example, CUE, EEF, and UNW are all engaged with various agencies in Jordan. This arrangement elevates the potential for the Program to have desired impact in that country. That said, the BHP Foundation did not prioritize geographic proximity when selecting partners, and there are no explicit plans thus far for formal cross-partner collaboration based on proximity. The BHP Foundation has, however, explicitly hypothesized that each partner's focus on particular decisionmakers and learners could lead to sharing of insights. For example, EEF's focus on teachers' and leaders' practices in formal schooling environments could lead to transferable knowledge for TFA, whose project aims to affect the work of community leaders, or for UNW, whose focus on training women occurs outside the formal classroom. Meanwhile, GBC-Ed fills a clear gap by targeting the corporate sector as a key actor whose investment and engagement decisions are consequential to moving the needle on global educational equity, and CUE's encompassing systems approach targets higher-level decisionmakers, such as government actors, funders, civil society, and teacher organizations. Building their understanding of and sense of urgency for the needs of decisionmakers on the ground (e.g., teachers) is essential for systemic change at scale.

In all, the BHP Foundation deliberately assembled these initiatives and partners not only for their individual strengths but also for their complementarity. Whether targeting teachers, community members, corporate actors, government actors, or stakeholders in other roles, partners' projects all involve working with people who help young people learn, supporting them to access and use information to improve educational quality and equity. In this respect, through its five partners, the BHP Foundation Program is exploring and sharing ideas for mobilizing actors and reaching learners across the landscape.

CHAPTER THREE

Measuring Progress

Good practice in program monitoring and evaluation includes prespecifying key indicators of progress toward program goals and tracking these indicators over the life of a program (Bamberger and Hewitt, 1986; Culbertson, Gonzalez, and Nanda, 2017; Haims et al., 2011; McDavid and Hawthorn, 2006). Indicators may be quantitative or qualitative, but either way, they should provide a reliable, objective means to measure whether progress toward goals has been achieved (Haims et al., 2011; U.S. Agency for International Development, 2009). As a component of the evaluation system of the BHP Foundation's Program, we developed a framework that links key indicators from the five partners' efforts to the activities and interim outcomes in the Program theory of change. These align with the work—and direct results of that work—expected to be achieved over the five years of the partners' projects.

Our indicator framework, depicted in Figure 3.1, assigns each key indicator to a particular step of the theory of change. However, the same indicator may measure multiple activities or multiple interim outcomes. We also identify which activities contribute to generating the interim outcomes being measured, although, of course, not every activity contributes to every outcome.

In general, we expect that long-term outcomes will take beyond the five years of the partners' work (and our evaluation) to achieve, and we do not explicitly map indicators from the partners to long-term outcomes. We describe how the BHP Foundation could gather indicators to shed light on whether the Program as a whole is making progress toward long-term outcomes.

Developing the Indicator Framework

To select the key indicators, we first compiled a library of more than 250 indicators that the partners were already planning to use to measure their own BHP Foundation efforts and mapped them to the Program theory of change. We then developed a shorter, targeted list of about 40 total indicators, with six to ten indicators for each partner. This was done through a two-step process. First, we developed an initial shortlist by analyzing the indicator library against SMART criteria. We prioritized the

Figure 3.1
Key Indicator Framework for the BHP Foundation Program Evaluation

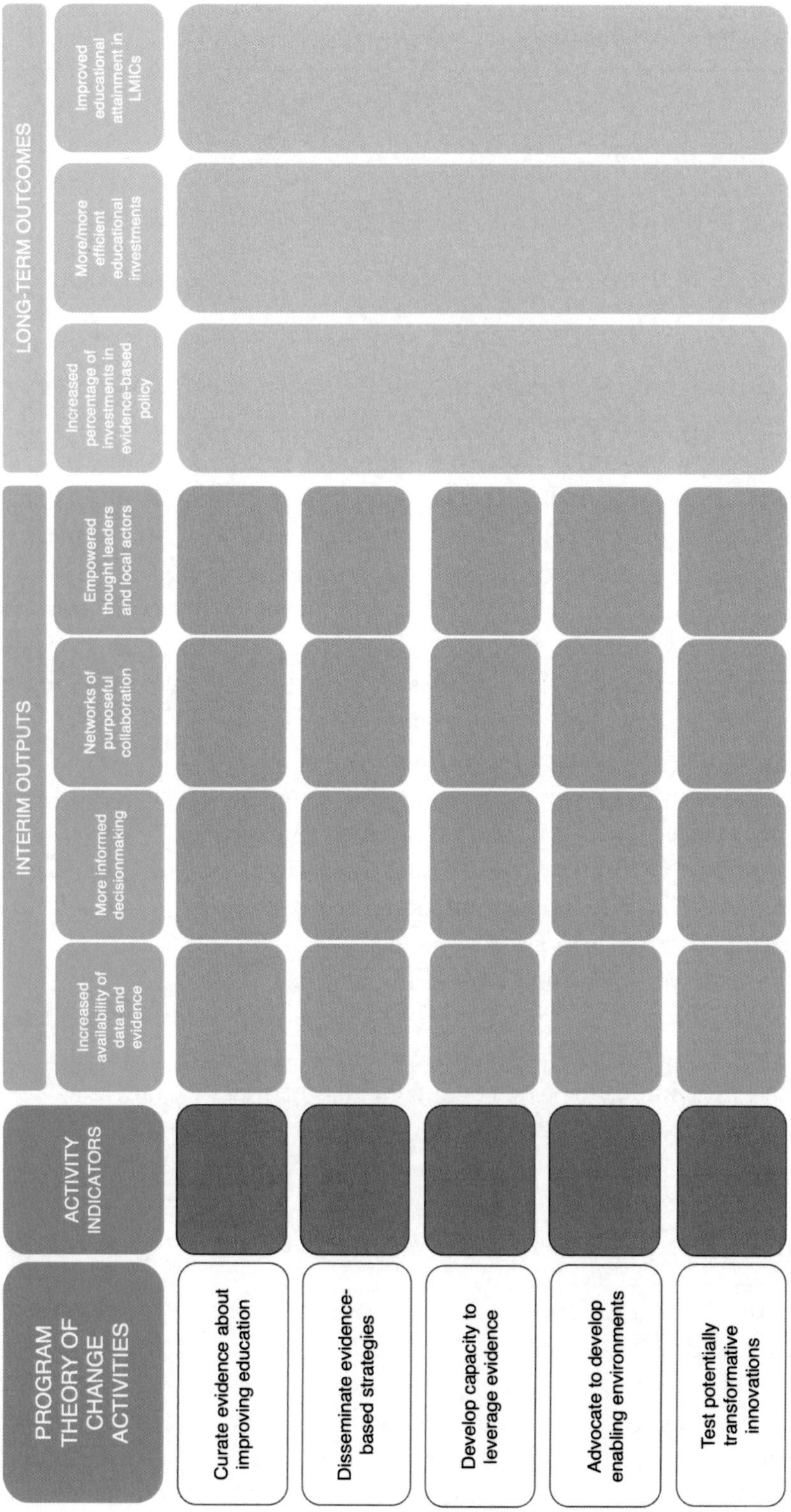

SOURCE: Copyright BHP Foundation; used with permission. LMIC = low- and middle-income countries.

appropriate criterion, seeking indicators with clear alignment to the BHP Foundation's theory of change and, therefore, the greatest importance in measuring how the theory of change is playing out across the five partner projects. We then sought indicators that met the other criteria of SMART—in short, clear, tangible indicators that can be measured objectively during our time-limited evaluation. We aimed for the list to (1) measure aspects of each partner's work that are central to that project's own theory of change, (2) link clearly to the activities and outcomes in the Program theory of change, and (3) meet SMART criteria. Second, we consulted with each partner to refine the indicators that best represented its work.

We note that, by design, each of the five partners operates at different places on the theory of change—engaging in different sets of activities aiming at different objectives. There is no expectation that each partner will collect indicators linked to every step of the theory of change. Moreover, even when partners are engaged in similar work, it is impossible to collect precisely the same indicators from each partner. Therefore, just as the Program consists of mutually reinforcing projects, the indicator framework should be viewed as an aggregation of key indicators that complement each other and collectively measure how the Program is progressing. It does not replace the individual monitoring and evaluation frameworks of the five partners, and it would be inappropriate and potentially misleading to measure any individual partner's effectiveness through this indicator framework.

Key Activity and Interim Outcome Indicators

Tables 3.1 and 3.2 show the numbers of key activity and interim outcome indicators selected for the indicator framework. These tables tabulate how many key indicators

Table 3.1
Number of Key Activity Indicators by Partner

Activity	CUE	EEF	GBC-Ed	TFA	UNW	Total
Curate evidence about improving education	3	2	1	3	2	11
Disseminate evidence-based strategies	6	2	1	4	1	14
Develop capacity to leverage evidence	3	2	1	3	1	10
Advocate to develop enabling environments	3	1	0	0	2	6
Test potentially transformative investments	0	1	0	0	3	4
Total (deduplicated)	6	5	2	5	5	23

Table 3.2
Number of Key Interim Outcome Indicators by Partner

Interim Outcome	CUE	EEF	GBC-Ed	TFA	UNW	Total
Increased availability of data and evidence	3	2	0	1	1	7
More-informed decisionmaking	0	2	2	1	1	6
Networks of purposeful collaboration	0	2	0	2	2	6
Empowered thought leaders and local actors	3	2	2	3	2	12
Total (deduplicated)	3	5	2	4	4	18

we selected from each partner, as well as for each activity and interim outcome in the Program theory of change. The counts in the tables reflect our mapping of indicators the partners were already planning to collect that clearly align to the activities and interim outcomes in the Program theory of change (and meet other SMART criteria; as described in the "Developing the Indicator Framework" section) to those activities and interim outcomes.[1] Box 3.1 shows a selection of these indicators; a full list of the indicators is in Appendix A.

In total, we selected 23 key activity indicators and 18 key interim outcome indicators across the five partners, with individual indicators often mapping to multiple activities or multiple outcomes. For example, an activity indicator might measure both disseminating evidence and developing capacity to leverage that evidence, while interim outcome indicators measuring networks might also signal progress toward empowered thought leaders and local actors to the extent that those networks incorporate those stakeholders.

We selected more key indicators for the first three activities of the BHP Foundation theory of change (curating and disseminating evidence and developing capacity), with fewer indicators for the fourth and fifth activities in the theory of change diagram (related to advocacy and testing innovations). This is because of the nature of the partners' work and the aspects of their work for which they track indicators. For example, CUE engages in curating and disseminating evidence, developing capacity to leverage evidence by building and sharing user-friendly tools, and engaging with policymakers and other stakeholders. TFA and GBC-Ed similarly focus on curating, disseminating, and developing capacity to use evidence. The key activity indicators for

---

[1] We note that the lines between activities and interim outcomes of those activities, as well as between the five activities and the four interim outcomes themselves, can blur. We sought to link the indicators to the stage of the theory of change (i.e., an indicator either measures activities *or* interim outcomes) and to the individual activities and interim outcomes for which they are most appropriate. Others may have broader or narrower conceptions of which indicators relate to which activities or interim outcomes.

Box 3.1. A Selection of the Indicators

Activity Indicators

CUE: Number of knowledge products (e.g., publications, tools, podcasts) developed by each workstream

EEF: Number of engagements with policymakers

GBC-Ed: Number of tools developed as prototypes and finalized

TFA: Number of Community Impact Lab learning experiences

UNW: Number of Women's Empowerment Hubs/community spaces

Interim Outcome Indicators

CUE: Number of externally initiated engagements, such as requests from the media, briefings, and panels

EEF: Number of organizations supported to take on the role of evidence brokers

GBC-Ed: Number of business users of tools

TFA: Share of participants in learning experiences reporting increased knowledge as a result

UNW: Number of employed/entrepreneur women among second chance education program graduates

EEF and UNW, in contrast, include indicators of testing potentially transformative investments, as these are core parts of their BHP Foundation–funded work.

Partners also varied in terms of which of their indicators map to which interim outcomes, reflecting the different objectives for the partners' projects, as well as which outcomes can be measured well. CUE, for example, quantifies externally initiated engagements, a signal that its knowledge products are getting traction among thought leaders, while drawing more heavily on qualitative examples to understand impacts in other domains. EEF's metrics span all four interim outcomes. TFA aims squarely at building out, strengthening, and sharing resources with its networks of partners and program alumni around the world. UNW seeks to empower women to pursue employment or entrepreneurial pathways, while its measurements of whether its efforts are effective contribute to increasing the availability of evidence about what works. GBC-Ed plans to track whether its tools are being used by private-sector actors and whether its efforts are changing the conversation about interacting with the private sector among noncorporate education stakeholders; both of these may be considered indicators of empowered thought leaders and more-informed decisionmaking.

Table 3.3 displays how these key interim outcome indicators link back to activities in the theory of change. Each cell in the table indicates which partners have a key interim outcome indicator that measures progress toward the interim outcome (in the

Table 3.3
Linking Key Interim Outcome Indicators to Activities

	Interim Outcome			
Activity	**Increased Availability of Data and Evidence**	**More-Informed Decisionmaking**	**Networks of Purposeful Collaboration**	**Empowered Thought Leaders and Local Actors**
Curate evidence about improving education	CUE; EEF; TFA; UNW	EEF; GBC-Ed; TFA	None	CUE; GBC-Ed; TFA; UNW
Disseminate evidence-based strategies	CUE; EEF; TFA	EEF; GBC-Ed; TFA; UNW	EEF; TFA	All partners
Develop capacity to leverage evidence	CUE; UNW	GBC-Ed; TFA	EEF; TFA; UNW	All partners
Advocate to develop enabling environments	CUE	EEF; GBC-Ed; UNW	None	CUE; EEF; GBC-Ed; UNW
Test potentially transformative investments	EEF; UNW	None	UNW	UNW

column) that flows from the activity (in the row). This presentation makes apparent the multiple pathways to interim outcomes, while also showing which pathways have the most partner involvement. For example, there are key interim outcome indicators from all five partners that measure progress toward "empowered thought leaders and local actors" resulting from the activity of "disseminate evidence-based strategies." Other pathways involving the activities of curating and disseminating evidence are similarly dense. There are fewer partners on other pathways, such as from the activity of "test potentially transformative investments" to the interim outcomes or from any of the activities to the interim outcome of "networks of purposeful collaboration."

Long-Term Outcome Indicators

Program activities and interim outcomes can be measured well over the five years of the partners' funded work by drawing on indicators from the partners, but this often is not the case for the long-term outcomes. This is to be expected given the time-limited nature of the partners' work and our evaluation, coupled with the longer time horizons needed to make progress toward the three long-term outcomes (increased share of investments in evidence-based policies; more and more-efficient educational investments; and improved educational attainment among the underrepresented, vulnerable, and marginalized). Importantly, for the purposes of the Program on the whole, the partners' ability to meet their objectives over the span of their projects might lay the groundwork for—but not necessarily indicate—longer-term Program-level success.

Going forward, we will work with the BHP Foundation to identify targeted *long-term outcome indicators* that it could track beyond the life of the current funded projects to enable continued evaluation of how the Program theory of change is playing out. These might include indicators from individual partners that provide an early signal of progress toward improved educational attainment, meaningful changes in policy or budgetary priorities, or shifts in investments toward evidence-based policies. With additional time and resources, partners could continue to monitor these indicators over the longer term. Long-term outcome indicators also might include indicators that reflect the results of the work of the partners in the collective, including their collaboration in support of Program goals. These indicators should be developed with an eye toward SMART criteria, as we have done for activity and interim outcome indicators. However, as the horizon shifts into the longer term, it becomes more likely that the most appropriate measures will be more qualitative in nature or draw on targeted, project- or jurisdiction-specific quantitative measures as part of a broader narrative that describes the contributions of the Program to long-term outcomes.

We further propose pairing these targeted measures designed to trace the impacts of Program activities from the near term into the longer term with monitoring high-level indicators of progress toward long-term outcomes in countries in which the Program is particularly active.

Of the hundreds of indicators tracked in relation to SDG4, our dashboard (Table 3.4) includes five that are widely collected across countries and that link to the desired long-term outcomes of the Program. We do not select SDG4 indicators to measure investments in evidence-based policies, nor do the measures of the volume of educational investments capture the efficiency of those investments. However, improvements in educational attainment could indicate that investments were grounded in evidence about how to achieve such improvements.

Table 3.4
Sustainable Development Goal 4 Long-Term Outcome Indicator Dashboard

Long-Term Outcome	Indicator
Improved educational attainment	• Persistence to last grade of primary school, by sex • Adolescents out of school (percentage of lower secondary school age), by sex • Youth literacy rate (percentage of people ages 15–24), by sex
More and more-efficient educational investments	• Government expenditure on education (percentage of gross domestic product) • Government expenditure on education (percentage of government expenditure)
Increased share of investments in evidence-based policies	• Not directly measured using SDG4 indicators

To keep attention on the longer-term vision of the BHP Foundation in improving education while simultaneously recognizing the localized nature of much of the partners' work, we plan to track these indicators for ten countries where multiple partners are engaged in meaningful work in connection with the Program. These ten countries are Australia, Cameroon, Chile, India, Jordan, Mexico, Peru, the Philippines, Spain, and the United Kingdom. Baseline measures on each of these indicators are included in Table A.10 in Appendix A. We would consider *positive movement over time* on these indicators, particularly *increases in the rate of improvement*, as suggesting progress toward the intended long-term outcomes. This is consistent with the approach suggested in the International Commission on Financing Global Education Opportunity's (2016) *The Learning Generation* report.

We stress that this dashboard is primarily descriptive. We cannot directly link the BHP Foundation or partner efforts to nation-level trends; in most cases, we would not expect the Program to substantially influence national trends within the time frame of our study, although the BHP Foundation is working toward contributing toward these goals. Moreover, many of these indicators are reported with a time lag, meaning that available data at the conclusion of the evaluation period would not reflect the full impacts over the duration of the BHP Foundation–funded project work. Nonetheless, monitoring these indicators can provide useful context for the BHP Foundation about the countries in which the Program is active and shed light on the challenges or opportunities that partners face in carrying out Program activities.

We also will explore opportunities to derive long-term outcome indicators from the World Bank's Systems Approach for Better Education Results (SABER) initiative, or related efforts. SABER uses data to characterize the strength of education systems around the world, including countries' education policies and institutions, with the goal of "allow[ing] education leaders and stakeholders to see inside the black box between education inputs and outcomes" (World Bank, 2013). Though its coverage to date in the countries where the partners are most active is limited, and it suffers from similar limitations as the SDG4 indicators with respect to time lag and difficulties of attributing impacts, SABER's goals and the data it collects are well aligned with the mechanisms through which the Program envisions achieving its long-term objectives. Therefore, measures from SABER for relevant countries merit consideration for inclusion among the targeted measures of long-term program contributions.

Figure 3.2 depicts our indicator framework in full, noting the number of key indicators for each activity in the theory of change and for each activity-to-outcome pathway and listing the names of the partners with indicators in each of the activity and interim outcome categories. The long-term outcome columns in the figure list the indicators in our SDG4 dashboard and note that these will be coupled with targeted selections of additional long-term outcome indicators.

Figure 3.2
Key Indicator Framework for the Program Evaluation: Number of SMART Indicators and Partners with Indicators

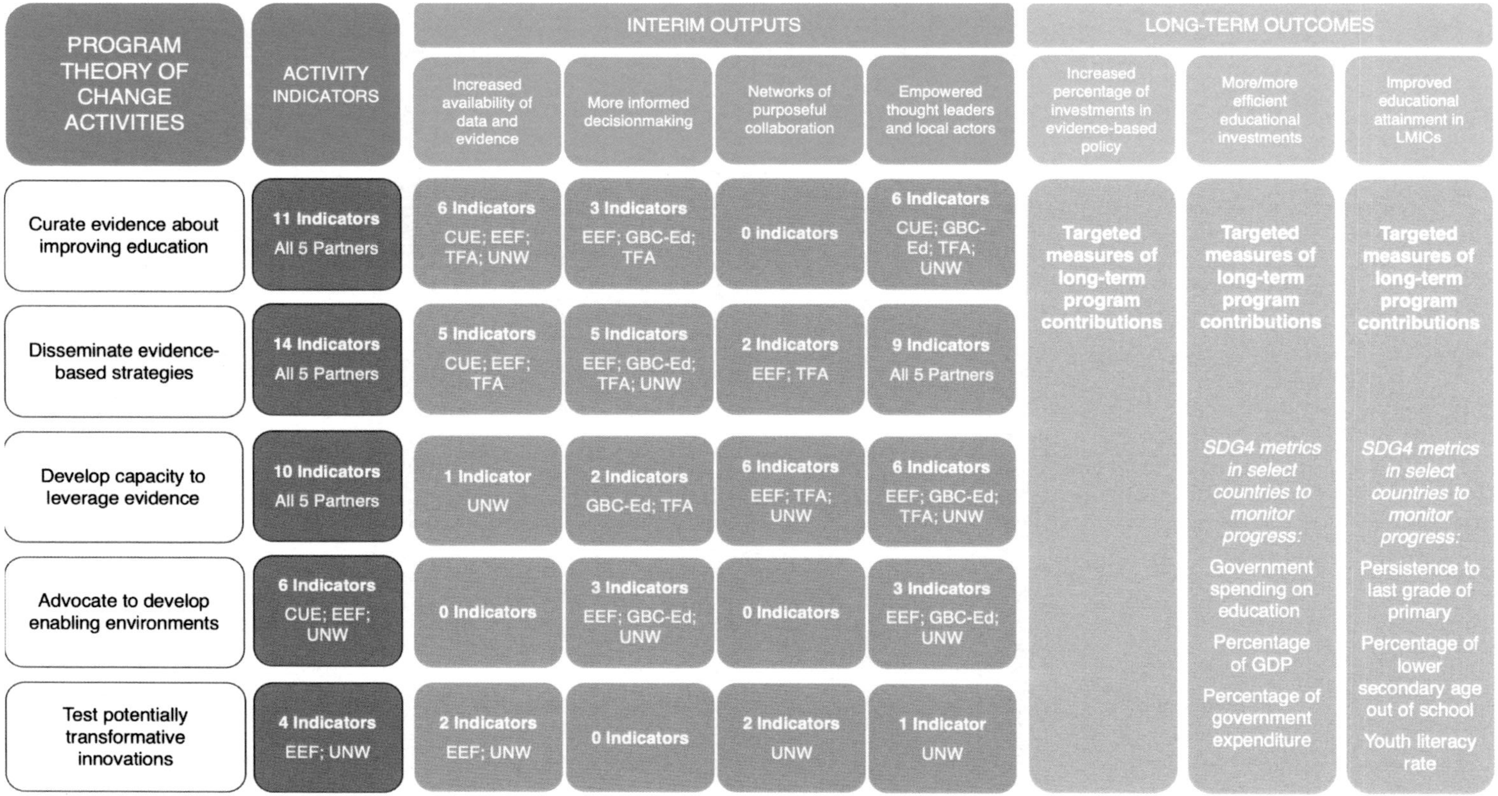

SOURCE: Copyright BHP Foundation; used with permission.

NOTES: Activity and interim outcome indicators are distinct measures. However, each interim outcome indicator is associated with one or more activity categories. Partners are listed in cells when at least one key indicator measures their work in that cell. GDP = gross domestic product. LMIC = low- and middle-income countries.

Defining Success Using the Key Indicators

In our evaluation, we will track the key indicators as a gauge of the success of the Program in comparison with the components of the theory of change. We will do so explicitly for activities and interim outcomes, where measurable progress is anticipated over the five years of our evaluation, and will report on long-term outcome measures as they are identified and to the extent that they can be captured over the span of our evaluation. Collectively, this analysis will trace the contribution of the partners' work to the long-term intended impacts of the Program by documenting the degree to which the partners' efforts yielded tangible results the theory of change considers to be critical precursors of the long-term outcomes.

To measure success, we first worked with the partners to identify whether there are target benchmarks for success for their BHP Foundation–funded work and, if so, what they are. Prespecifying targets is much more likely for activity indicators than for interim outcome indicators, although even for activities there are many indicators for which targets are not set. Advocacy activity indicators (e.g., meetings with policymakers or other stakeholders) are the least likely to have prespecified targets; indicators of testing transformative investments are the most likely to have such targets. Comparing progress with prespecified targets will factor into the assessment, but we recognize that quantitative targets are only part of the picture, and that it is not always feasible or meaningful to pre-specify targets. Moreover, while the indicators documented in the partners' reporting to the BHP Foundation reflects work accomplished over the time span of their BHP Foundation funding, the partners often draw on other resources to support their work, and we generally will not be able to isolate the results of the BHP Foundation funding.

During the evaluation, we will assign each indicator a value of zero to three that assesses the degree to which the partner met benchmarks for success. To assign these values, we will draw on data provided by the partners and discuss with them where they believed they met or fell short of their objectives as measured by the indicators. Although we *quantify* success in the form of a zero to three rating, there is a degree of *qualitative* judgment that informs the ratings. Table 3.5 lists these ratings and how they are defined.

For each of the five activities and four interim outcomes, we will construct two versions of a success index by rolling up the individual indicator ratings. The first approach will weight each indicator equally, through a simple average. The second approach will weight each partner with indicators for that activity or interim outcome equally by first averaging across indicators for each partner (if there are multiple key indicators tracked by that partner) and then averaging the partners' scores together. We expect that these two approaches will yield complementary information about how the activities and outcomes played out across BHP Foundation investments.

We will develop a similar set of success indexes for the pathways to outcomes by averaging the ratings across indicators of interim outcomes that result from each activity. This analysis will complement the individual activity and outcome analyses by

Table 3.5
Key Indicator Rating Rubric

Rating	Types of Results That Would Yield Rating
Zero: Not successful	• Unable to track or report indicator • Activity or interim outcome measured by indicator did not take place
One: Partially successful with significant shortcomings	• Meaningful difficulties tracking or reporting indicator such that it is not a reliable measure of progress • Fell well short of prespecified target for indicator or little movement on indicator without a target
Two: Mostly successful with some shortcomings	• Generally able to reliably track and report indicator • Fell short of prespecified target for indicator in some dimension or generally positive but inconsistent movement on indicator without a target
Three: Fully successful	• Always able to reliably track and report indicator • Clearly met or exceeded prespecified targets or demonstrated clear, consistent positive movement on indicator without a target

NOTE: The ability to reliability track and report on an indicator to the degree specified by each rating is necessary but not sufficient to earn that rating; for example, an indicator that can generally or always be tracked but that fell well short of a prespecified target or showed little movement likely would earn a one rather than a two or three.

quantifying whether certain activities are more likely to yield measurable success on outcome indicators than other activities.

Reporting to Date on Key Indicators

The tables in Appendix A list each key activity and interim outcome indicator we will track along with its prespecified target (if any) and status as reported by the partners. Although we do not provide success ratings in this baseline report, reporting an indicator's status demonstrates that the partner is in fact able to collect and report the indicator and signals that the project is conducting the specified activities and starting to yield measurable outcomes. Tables 3.6 and 3.7 show our findings for activity and

Table 3.6
Key Activity Indicators: Preliminary Metrics

Activity	Number of Indicators	Number with Target	Number Reported Status
Curate evidence about improving education	11	7	11
Disseminate evidence-based strategies	14	8	13
Develop capacity to leverage evidence	10	6	9
Advocate to develop enabling environments	6	2	6
Test potentially transformative investments	4	4	4

Table 3.7
Key Interim Outcome Indicators: Preliminary Metrics

Interim Outcome	Number of Indicators	Number With Target	Number Reported Status
Increased availability of data and evidence	7	1	4
More-informed decisionmaking	6	3	2
Networks of purposeful collaboration	6	3	5
Empowered thought leaders and local actors	12	5	8

interim outcome indicators, respectively. Most activity indicators have been reported to date, while fewer interim outcome indicators have. In particular, indicators of more-informed decisionmaking are unlikely to have been reported to date.

Summary and Next Steps

We developed an indicator framework for the Program that maps a selection of key indicators the partners are already collecting for the purposes of their individual projects to the activities and interim outcomes for the Program on the whole. We will monitor these key indicators over the course of our evaluation and will use a categorical rating rubric to assess the degree to which partners were successful in conducting the activities or achieving interim outcomes as measured by the indicators. We will analyze findings by activity, interim outcome, and pathway to interim outcome to show where partners in the aggregate were more or less successful. These analyses will shed light on whether the Program is yielding the interim outcomes the BHP Foundation views as critical precursors of long-term change. Moving forward, we aim to work with the BHP Foundation to identify targeted indicators connected to the long-term outcomes that the Program seeks to influence. Importantly, we expect that indicators of long-term success will involve pairing select quantitative metrics with rich, qualitative narratives that trace the contributions of the Program toward the intended long-term outcomes. Capturing the richer narrative of how the partners are carrying out their work is the subject of the next chapter.

CHAPTER FOUR

Illustrating Partner Activities, Challenges, and Lessons Learned

As presented in Chapter Three, the indicator component of the evaluation will be used to report to what extent the Program is making progress toward targets, and the qualitative research component will be used to report on what the work that partners undertook looks like and what facilitated or challenged this work. Through generating qualitative insights of Program partners' activities, we seek to help the BHP Foundation and the field of education as a whole understand the pathways by which the Program is affecting education and learning globally.

In this chapter, we first illustrate the types of activities partners have undertaken. We then summarize some common challenges that the partners faced and lessons learned to date that could inform the next phase of work. We provide brief examples in text boxes to make concrete some general trends. As with the examples presented in Chapter Two, these examples are not intended to provide a comprehensive inventory of all activities partners are engaged in. We will track these and other emergent examples throughout the five years of the evaluation. Finally, we preview the next steps we will take to more deeply understand the pathways of impact. The findings in this section are informed by analysis of our interviews and of quarterly and annual reports that the partners submitted to the BHP Foundation (see Appendix B for details of the qualitative research approach).

Examples of Partner Activities

In this section, we highlight some early and planned undertakings across the five funded partners with respect to the five activities identified in the Program's theory of change. Most partners were engaged in related work long before receiving BHP Foundation funding, but our discussion focuses on their efforts since launching their BHP Foundation–funded projects (since 2018 for most partners) that are directly connected to those projects. In line with our overall study approach, we do not evaluate each partner's contribution individually but rather speak to broad themes across partners' work.

Curate Evidence About Improving Education

Collectively, as part of BHP Foundation–funded activities, partners have curated evidence or generated new knowledge about a range of practices that could improve education. Such activities suggest progress toward the first target interim outcome of increasing availability of data and evidence. Partners have identified evidence through several strategies, as shown in Box 4.1, and have largely employed three strategies to enhance the evidence base. The first strategy involves a form of curation—reviewing existing evidence or conducting metaresearch. The second strategy involves data gathering, primarily through surveys or interviews with experts and stakeholders. The third strategy involves studying implementation of practices in the field.

Disseminate Evidence-Based Strategies

Since receiving BHP Foundation funding, partners have disseminated evidence-based strategies in various ways and forums and, in doing so, have contributed to the target

Box 4.1. Partners Employed Three Primary Strategies to Curate or Generate Evidence

1. Review existing research or conduct metaresearch

CUE and its partners will synthesize evidence related to "how educational technologies can help improve teaching and learning across the developing world" (CUE, 2020). EEF has already "unzipped" and examined thousands of studies in the Teaching and Learning Toolkit for context- and target-group–specific evidence of how particular strategies support student achievement. These strategies range in topics, including feedback practices, collaborative learning, metacognition, and behavioral interventions.

2. Gather original data

CUE is working to document essential features of user-friendly real-time data collection tools in education by surveying the developers of such systems. CUE will also gather data from parents and teachers to inform how parents can take part in systemic reforms through increased demand for innovative pedagogies. GBC-Ed has begun engaging third parties to identify how businesses and enterprises of different sizes are supporting and affecting global education.

3. Study implementation of practices in the field

For two years, through its Scaling Labs initiative, CUE examined scaling practices and processes in five countries as members of the lab worked to articulate a scaling vision, develop scaling plans for an educational intervention, and iteratively implement their plan using data to drive decisionmaking. Through this initiative, CUE derived key scaling principles and illustrated what they look like in practice. Similarly, TFA studied community impact initiatives in 11 communities to generate learnings about the drivers of community impact.

interim outcome of increasing the availability of data and evidence about what works to improve education globally (see Figure 2.1). A prominent dissemination approach in this respect is publishing reports, policy briefs, and commentaries that synthesize insights gained from curating evidence. Partners, including TFA and UNW, found case studies of implementing partners to be particularly compelling. Partners have also used podcasts, videos, and websites to disseminate learning. One common approach is holding large-scale convenings and workshops with funders, policymakers, and other stakeholders. Beyond broadcasting lessons, these events serve to establish networks that could further the impact of the work. Another prominent dissemination strategy involves developing public goods in the form of practical guidance and tools that support decisionmakers in applying lessons learned. The products have the potential to lead to a second target interim outcome—more-informed decisionmaking—as the projects mature. Box 4.2 provides some examples of such knowledge products.

Box 4.2. Partners Are Working Toward Developing Tools and Guidance to Support Decisionmaking as Part of Their Dissemination Strategy

By the first quarter of 2021, EEF aims to produce updated Teaching and Learning Toolkits with user-friendly brief summaries of interventions, identifying their effectiveness for certain student populations and contexts. Such products are intended to support practitioners (i.e., teachers and school leaders) in selecting evidence-based strategies to bolster student achievement.

Meanwhile, GBC-Ed is solidifying plans to develop and eventually pilot practical tools that will help businesses make strategic investments that contribute to SDG4.

CUE recently began developing a tool that provides guidance around scaling, supporting intervention adopters and implementers to think through key questions and identify factors in the environment that may enable or hinder scaling. CUE also plans to develop a repository of real-time data collection tools to support users to choose a tool with necessary features to meet their needs. A third CUE tool will help system leaders estimate costs associated with program implementation and scaling. CUE's eventual playbooks on how to effectively leverage educational technologies and on parent demand for education innovation also fall into this.

UN Women is developing products to document the evidence base of the global model of second chance education and tools to support eventual program scale-up. These products include a literature review of second chance education best practices, an Second Chance Education Programme operational manual, a handbook for establishing and running Second Chance Education Programme hubs, and a facilitator guide.

Develop Capacity to Leverage Evidences

Under the BHP Foundation program, funded partners have been developing their local partners' capacity to leverage evidence. Three key strategies for doing so have emerged. One approach involves facilitating peer-to-peer, network-based sharing of learning. Another related strategy involves engaging target implementers to provide guidance early in the tool development process. A third strategy involves seeding a funding mechanism that supports the generation of evidence and rigorous testing of innovations and, in doing so, acculturating the partner organizations to this practice. Box 4.3 provides examples of each of these strategies. In the long term, these efforts are expected to lead to more-empowered local actors and thought leaders who will have the knowledge, inclination, and capacity to make decisions about education programs and policy that are informed by evidence.

Conduct Advocacy to Develop Enabling Environments

At this early stage, partners largely conceived of activities in this realm not as explicitly advocating for policy changes. Instead, activities would build relationships with country partners and raise awareness of the need for equitable educational opportunities and evidence-based practices to improve educational attainment of vulnerable populations. To these ends, partners have visited with ministers of education and other policymakers across their partner sites. They have also reached out to such international and intergovernmental organizations as the OECD and UNESCO. TFA has begun exploratory conversations with members of the OECD about how to advance education policy and reform and sustainable development. Box 4.4 highlights the work UNW has done in the area of awareness-raising and fostering environments for meaningful policy change.

Test Potentially Transformative Investments

Since beginning their BHP Foundation–funded work, partners have pursued activities related to testing potentially transformative practices. EEF's initiative to test promising practices is the Global Trials Fund. EEF has commissioned two rounds of RCTs, although this initiative has been subject to challenges, as detailed in "Shared Challenges and Lessons Learned." Results of the trials are not yet available, but they are expected to add to the global evidence base about what works to improve education, particularly in low- and middle-income countries. Meanwhile, most of UNW's local partners have launched the Second Chance Education Programme and the Women's Empowerment Hubs in which the program would be administered; however, the outbreak of coronavirus disease 2019 (COVID-19) halted progress. UNW has documented the number of women accessing the hubs, providing preliminary evidence of a promising intervention in which women complete various courses and learning pathways; grow in skills, confidence, and agency; and attain gainful employment.

Box 4.3. Partners Are Building Their Local Partners' Capacity to Leverage Evidence Through Three Main Strategies

1. Facilitate peer-to-peer learning networks

TFA's Community Impact Lab is a prime example of a network used to share learning and build capacity. It has hosted multiple experiences, including workshops, learning loops (in which participants join to gather new ideas and practices, apply them in their contexts, and return to share lessons learned), roundtables, and consulting-like sessions (in which Community Impact Lab leaders support local leaders as they implement a project). The primary targets of these activities are staff members in TFA partner organizations and alumni leaders actively working to foster community progress.

CUE's scaling labs are another example of peer-to-peer learning to support the development of local capacity to use evidence. A community of practice has emerged from these labs that engages in regular knowledge exchange and collaborative problem-solving. An webinar for the community will focus on how to engage government partners in the scaling process. Such activities could empower thought leaders and local actors in the years to come.

2. Engage target implementers early

GBC-Ed assembled a Guidance Group of about 30 senior leaders of companies that were already actively supporting education. The initial and primary charge of this group is to provide input into the direction of GBC-Ed's project, including feedback on prototype tools and products. This early engagement is expected to build into these businesses receiving first-available training to deploy and test the tools and products. GBC-Ed is cultivating these partners' buy-in and capacity to implement products by engaging them from the beginning.

3. Provide seed funding

EEF designed the matched funding requirement for its Global Trials Fund to increase local ownership and partner investment in the practice of commissioning and funding trials. EEF has encountered challenges related to the trials; nevertheless, some of its partners have begun the work with EEF's guidance. The trials are intended to stimulate the local evaluation markets. To build evaluative capacity, EEF has appointed an experienced outside evaluator and will seek to integrate local researchers on the team to develop their skills and knowledge.

Meanwhile, through its Community Impact Fund, TFA has awarded over ten short-term small-scale grants to local partners to allow them to test whether their leadership development practices helped build the capacities of local leaders. The financial support was designed both to generate additional evidence-based insights for TFA and to encourage locally led experimentation and learning.

Box 4.4. UN Women Has Taken Steps to Foster an Enabling Environment for Sustained Programming and Policy Change

UNW's approach to advocacy and policy influence begins with trying to raise awareness and initiate cooperation and dialogue at a local level, then expanding outward. Building broad, strong partnerships with public and private sectors—engaging government and grassroots organizations, employers, and civil society allies—is fundamental to UNW's overall strategy. These partnerships not only help develop local buy-in and infrastructure for sustaining and scaling the Second Chance Education Programme but also help shape attitudes, behaviors, and policies that further women's educational and career opportunities.

UNW has partnered with local governments where desirable and possible—for example, in Mexico—to open Women's Empowerment Hubs. These partnerships secure government commitment to helping women create agency and bettering their educational and personal outcomes. In Mexico, UNW is deeply engaged in awareness-raising; for example, it has worked with municipal government officials to help them understand how employment site postings can be made more gender-inclusive and welcoming of women applicants.

Shared Challenges and Lessons Learned

Several common challenges hampered BHP Foundation–funded partners' work during 2019 and 2020. These challenges fall roughly into three categories: those pertaining to local or implementing partners, those related to the greater context in which the project work is situated, and those related to the COVID-19 global health crisis. Lessons learned from these challenges facilitate continued efforts.

Challenges and Lessons Related to Local Implementing Partners

In the first category, multiple partners expressed concern about the *readiness of local partner organizations* and stakeholders to implement certain project initiatives or embrace transformative educational change. The issue was evident in the reporting of CUE and EEF. Both organizations had curated or established evidence-based practices that they were eager to scale (e.g., CUE's catalog of effective education innovations and EEF's Evidence Hubs); however, in 2019, their first project year, both CUE and EEF regarded stakeholders' appetite and readiness to lead reform efforts as challenges to overcome in order to affect systemic change. CUE noted that a mindset shift toward systems thinking is required among some decisionmakers to help them adopt educational innovations. CUE is working to incorporate systems thinking in its work, and consultations with stakeholders help ensure that its tools and other products will support decisionmakers to apply CUE recommendations. Box 4.5 provides the example of

EEF facing and mitigating local partners' reluctance to establish Evidence Hubs, a key component of its project for the BHP Foundation Program.

Partners' readiness to implement may be low, but their interest in BHP Foundation–funded work was not. In fact, some partners faced the challenge of *having to handle high interest in and demand around their work.* Multiple partners reported high stakeholder engagement in multiple streams of their work, evidencing widespread interest in guidance around effective education innovations and practices. These partners had to consider, however, how (or to what extent) to meet the demand without overstretching their organizational capacity. See Box 4.6 for an example concerning CUE.

A related consideration around meeting increased demand was how to balance the desire for wide reach and large-scale impact with the commitment to cultivating

Box 4.5. Education Endowment Foundation Demonstrated Relevance of Evidence Hubs to Local Partners

Some partners were reluctant to create an Evidence Hub to generate, test, and support promising teaching practices that are based on the Research School Network in England. EEF reported that partners struggled to see the need for such hubs or to regard them as a key mechanism for translating evidence to practice.

To mitigate this challenge, EEF identified "hooks" in each partner country to introduce the idea of the Evidence Hub or connect it to existing structures that could play the role of a hub. In Spain, for example, EEF's partner, La Caixa Banking Foundation, is funding small-scale evaluations of promising education interventions. EEF now works with La Caixa to provide lessons about evidence-informed practices to teachers and leaders. EEF does so with toolkits and other resources it is co-developing with La Caixa. In essence, EEF is developing capacity for evidence use among the teachers that La Caixa that was already working with. EEF leadership believes that tapping into existing structures—rather than creating new ones—will be effective in mobilizing local jurisdictions.

Box 4.6. Center for Universal Education Strategized Around Meeting High Demand for Its Work and Technical Assistance

CUE received multiple requests from various jurisdictions (e.g., ministries of education, Global Partnership for Education) seeking support for implementing the key ideas of leapfrogging and scaling. Demand for technical assistance from Scaling Labs partners is also high.

CUE aims to share requested information with interested organizations without taxing its own staff by publishing and widely disseminating playbooks of promising innovations and growing lab partners' capacity.

relationships with existing local partners. EEF established international partnerships so quickly in 2019 and had so many demands to expand into additional jurisdictions that it had to reassess its growth strategy. Finally, in consultation with the BHP Foundation, EEF decided to stop exploring additional partnerships in 2020. Factoring into the decision was the recognition that taking on additional partners risked diluting the impact of its work with the original partners and might jeopardize reach project goals in those contexts. Strengthening the existing network of partners seemed to be a more prudent decision. Meanwhile, as Box 4.7 shows, TFA made a different calculation.

A third challenge pertains to local partners' capacity. Two BHP Foundation–funded partners expressed concerns along these lines. EEF experienced this in relation to a particular initiative—the Global Trials Fund. Box 4.8 provides details of this example.

More generally, UNW initially faced limitations in identifying implementation partners for its Second Chance Education Programme. The organization faced challenges in finding country-based partners that represented local populations, had experience in serving the education needs of adult women, and also had the infrastructure for setting up training centers. In the end, UNW explored relationships with a range of institutions, including local governments, education institutions, and the private sector. In addition, UNW took time to cultivate the interest and trust of potential partner organizations. Capacity challenges often persisted after program rollout. Second Chance Education Programme facilitators, for example, lacked the high level of digital literacy needed to support the learning of attendees, particularly in the context of COVID-19.

Partners reported that *developing and maintaining strong relationships* with local partners and stakeholders, including one-to-one relationships with individuals in the network, has helped to ensure progress in the face of these challenges. They also appreciated the driving force of a *shared vision and passion* among team members and many local partners for the work. While good intentions and shared ambitions are critical, they do not in themselves overcome local capacity limitations. As a result, partners realized that an essential component of their work involved building the general capacity of their local partners, not just their capacity to leverage evidence, as identified in the theory of change. Partners increasingly attended to this by offering trainings, workshops, learning and sharing sessions, and coaching.

Box 4.7. Teach for All Expanded Engagement with Partner Sites

TFA highlighted a potential risk of engaging closely with only a limited number of partner sites: missing out on potential lessons from promising sites that are not as closely monitored or do not have as close a relationship with the lead organization. As a result of this realization, TFA aimed to engage more widely with all of its Community Impact Innovation Partners across the network on a regular basis. This would enable it to better identify cases of community progress to learn from and sites that would benefit from greater support (TFA, 2019).

Box 4.8. Education Endowment Foundation Adjusted Its Global Trials Fund Initiative

EEF documented partner-related capacity challenges in commissioning Global Trials of promising interventions. These included securing the required matched funding component; understanding the "complexity around commissioning, designing, and implementing trials" (EEF, 2020); and finding local evaluators with the capacity to conduct high-quality trials. The challenges led to delays in commissioning trials and a smaller number of trials than planned.

EEF adjusted two aspects of the Global Trials. First, it reduced the matched funding requirement from 50 percent to 30 percent, which partners agreed is more feasible. Second, it will allow pilot evaluations (smaller and more preliminary in nature) and will support partners in understanding the criteria for such pilots. Furthermore, EEF is looking to leverage the success of its fellowship program, possibly developing fellows' evaluation capacity to fill the gap.

Challenges and Lessons Related to Broader Context

Underlying some of the challenges centered on local partners are complex issues in the broader context in which the project work is situated. One specific issue is the perceived lack of system readiness or a lack of a culture of readiness for innovations and transformative change. EEF, for example, noted that, in partner countries, funding RCTs was essentially a new practice, just as it was novel to the English education system about a decade ago. As such, there will be a steep learning and capacity curve while local partners and the country at large learn to engage in and support the practice. More generally, for historical, political, and other reasons, country partners may hold an expectation that change in practice typically happens or ought to happen a certain way (e.g., by a policy mandate), which runs counter to the ground-up approach of the BHP Foundation–funded projects. This culture is admittedly difficult to change, but such a shift is likely necessary for meaningful change in the education system to occur.

A rapidly changing or instable political landscape, with turnover in leadership or shifts in funding priorities, also disrupted multiple partners' work. This included CUE's Real-Time Scaling Lab work in Tanzania and Botswana. Similarly, as described in Box 4.9, UNW contended with delays in implementation of the Second Chance Education Programme because of civil and political issues and processes. These circumstances led the partners to reflect on the reality of working to effect change in systems around the world and the importance of responding with agility and resilience, and with an eye toward identifying opportunities within seemingly indomitable challenges.

One realization that partners arrived at was the importance of learning about and taking into account the landscape in which they work and adjusting project strategies as needed. This includes seeking to understand the context, history, and structures of each partner jurisdiction and following the lead of local partners. Jurisdictions may

Box 4.9. UN Women Delayed Program Start Because of Challenges in Country Context, Using Time for Planning

Implementation of the Second Chance Education Programme was delayed in Chile because of civil unrest from October to December 2019. In consultation with its local partners, UNW decided that it was too risky to proceed with the launch of course offerings, so it delayed implementation to 2020. Similarly, program implementation in Jordan was postponed due to a delay in the country's approval process for humanitarian response activities. In both cases, project teams utilized the time gained as a result of the delay to plan detailed steps in preparation for full implementation (UNW, 2020).

start from very different points with respect to their understanding of the role of evidence, readiness for transformative change, expectations about how change occurs, and capacity to drive reform. Learning to work with existing structures and systems, rather than against them, has been an effective approach. The lead of a BHP Foundation–funded partner expressed this: "You can get further faster by finding similar things and attaching to them rather than imposing a different way of working." UNW seemed to adhere to this idea through using different models of operation for Women's Empowerment Hubs depending on the country context and organizational capacity. For example, in some jurisdictions, the local partner is a large organization; in other places, it is a government agency. The strategy of understanding local context and leveraging local expertise supports buy-in and aligns with a participatory approach that some BHP Foundation–funded partners argue is necessary for creating systemic change; local partners are given the opportunity to voice their needs and lead rather than have initiatives be imposed on them.

Considerations of context are also important because intended beneficiaries of programs and activities may have different needs from each other and from what is presumed. UNW, for example, noted that the needs assessments that it conducted early on were critical to helping validate the Second Chance Education Programme's theory of change and understanding in a nuanced way the needs and challenges facing women in each country so that the program could design effective learning content and pathways that avoid or dismantle specific barriers (UNW, 2019). TFA acknowledged the contextual nature of community impact but also understood that a common body of knowledge and practices can be captured and shared across sites to underlie the work. See Box 4.10 for an example with respect to GBC-Ed's work.

Challenges and Lessons Related to Coronavirus Disease 2019

The worldwide outbreak of COVID-19 in the first quarter of 2020 posed significant challenges for all partners, forcing them to pause, rescope, and/or pivot their work. Out of this situation emerged the lesson that partners needed to *be prepared, flexible, and responsive to emerging challenges,* to discover and seize the underlying opportunities that unforeseeable circumstances may present.

First, the pandemic led partners to rethink internal operations. For example, GBC-Ed changed its job description and approach to hiring key positions. Because of travel constraints, CUE revised the data collection methodology for one strand of its work, opting for virtual surveys, interviews, and focus groups instead of in-person data collection. CUE reported that this move, in fact, expanded the scope of its research, as it enabled the team to gather insights from a wider range of countries and stakeholder networks. Second, COVID-19–induced lockdowns and restrictions threatened on-the-ground implementation. Box 4.11 elaborates upon the case of UNW.

Third, COVID-19 exacerbated some existing inequities and brought to the fore even more urgent needs in certain countries and communities, leading BHP Foundation–funded partners and their local partners to shift their focus or expand their strategies. CUE, for example, accelerated its work on curating evidence-based practices related to educational technology and parent engagement. UNW noted that,

Box 4.10. Global Business Coalition for Education Learned the Importance of Understanding the Landscape for Planning

GBC-Ed learned early on the importance of speaking with stakeholders representing a wide range of business entities from different parts of the world—not only with Fortune 500 companies. It realized that there were no single straightforward answers about what all businesses needed in particular contexts to support decisionmaking around investing in education. The responses gathered from these conversations depend largely on businesses' context and characteristics and reveal a range of needs and solutions.

Box 4.11. UN Women Pivoted Program Delivery in the Face of Coronavirus Disease 2019–Induced Restrictions, Which Led to Challenges and Opportunities

Worldwide, the operation of UNW's Empowerment Hubs nearly came to a full stop because of COVID-19–related restrictions. To the extent possible, jurisdictions pivoted to delivering online learning to continue offering women content and programming to move their education forward. This shift presented challenges and opportunities of its own. For instance, after COVID-19 eases, the new modality could continue and be efficiently scaled to benefit a greater number of women; however, UNW also realized that the low level of digital literacy of its target beneficiaries was a barrier to progress and attainment of the organization's goals. As a result, UNW is considering diversifying its target audience to include more women with higher levels of digital literacy and general literacy.

in Mexico, the impact of COVID-19 on the economy will further threaten women's livelihood and social security; moreover, violence against women increased during COVID-19–related lockdowns. In Box 4.12, we illustrate some of the context-related challenges that TFA and its local partners navigated during the time of COVID-19.

All partners reported losing momentum for their projects because of COVID-19. However, they also found ways to move forward, innovating and leveraging networks to collaborate on solutions to COVID-19–induced educational problems, and using the moment to urge stakeholders to attend to educational inequities worldwide. Some of the pivots partners have made—toward virtual data collection and convenings and expanding target beneficiaries of programs—could very well contribute to the direction and impact of the project as a whole. These pivots also demonstrated the capacity of the partners and the educational system more broadly to adapt quickly and cut through barriers that might otherwise have stifled change. The postcrisis moment, when it arrives, could afford additional opportunities to shift policy and practice in new, evidence-based directions, by preserving and expanding upon crisis-era innovations.

Summary

Since receiving BHP Foundation funding, the five partners collectively have undertaken or have planned efforts in each of the five activity areas identified in the Pro-

Box 4.12. Teach for All Pivoted Its Work to Include a Focus on Responding to the Pandemic

During the COVID-19 crisis, communities in which TFA partner organizations operated experienced a cascade of challenges. School closures led to lack of learning opportunities for many children, as well as an increase in children experiencing hunger, abuse, or other threats to their well-being. These circumstances forced organizations to consider the balance between focusing on the planned work and responding to pressing needs.

Many partner communities prioritized supporting children and families' well-being, which, in turn, would support students' abilities to learn. TFA recognized that such work could help illuminate the conditions that enable community impact and strengthen the argument for strong local leadership. While it continued its planned activities, TFA shifted its focus to community responses and planned to publish a paper on the conditions that allow learning to continue during crises. The Community Impact Lab also pivoted the support it provided to partners and alumni to address timely questions around teaching and serving during the pandemic—for example, by creating forums for sharing learning and collaborative problem-solving.

gram's theory of change. They have employed strategies to curate evidence or generate new knowledge about a range practices that can improve education and are working to synthesize that knowledge into user-friendly, accessible tools and products that support decisionmaking. Anticipating the need, partners are building their local partners' capacity to leverage evidence in establishing policies and practice. They are also initiating conversations and building relationships designed to foster an enabling environment for long-term policy change. Finally, some partners are directly testing potentially transformative programs and practices. Although factors related to implementing partner capacity, the greater context, and COVID-19 challenged their efforts in these early year, the five funded partners have learned that focusing on relationships and capacity building, leaning into supportive structures, and being agile can propel the work.

Next Steps in Understanding Partners' Activities and Contributions

To deepen our understanding of how the theory of change underlying the BHP Foundation's investment may be playing out in the partners' work, in the next phase of our evaluation we will conduct a series of case studies that will serve over time to illustrate the pathways to change we have theorized, as well as the challenges along those pathways. Case studies will be based on discussions with partners and review of relevant materials. The focus of the case studies will be informed in part by the early findings above and determined in collaboration with the partners and the BHP Foundation.

In our current view, the case studies may take a few different forms. They may

- attend to a specific initiative within a partner's project (e.g., trace the pathway from identifying a promising evidence-based practice through the capacity development and dissemination work needed for it to yield impacts)
- explore a theme, issue, or question that affects multiple partners' work and is critical to progress (e.g., how to build a foundation and foster conditions for local policy change)
- focus on a geographical region in which multiple partners are seeking to improve educational opportunities (e.g., document contextual conditions that partners perceive as supporting or hindering progress and strategies they have employed to leverage or navigate the conditions to effect change).

We will synthesize this information to describe the narrative arc and implementation of these pathway initiatives to draw broad lessons learned. Analysis will be aimed at testing the assumptions underlying our theory of change and identifying promising practices with respect to each step in our theory of change. For example, case narratives can help illustrate whether the evidence and research being applied are scalable and have the potential to be catalytic, whether investments in capacity building are sufficient and which types of capacity building are most essential to success, and whether and how the results of local efforts are successfully leveraged to enhance broader adoption of best practices, as well as provide general insights about implementation facilitators and barriers. We expect that the case studies will provide lessons for the funded partners, the BHP Foundation's strategic network, and, potentially, the field at large.

CHAPTER FIVE

Visualizing Networks

As discussed in Chapter Two, networks of stakeholders are a critical type of capacity building with respect to the BHP Foundation's Program goals. Increasing the use of evidence in education depends on diffusion of innovation, organizational collaboration, and dissemination of best practices. These processes, in turn, rely on relationships, interactions, and the transmission of information or resources among networks of people or organizations. In line with this observation, many of the Program-funded partners are engaged in developing purposeful networks to facilitate their evidence-to-practice work. Research has shown that thinking strategically and intentionally about network development efforts can enhance policy impact (Leonardi and Contractor, 2018; Cross and Thomas, 2011).

We include an examination of networks in our evaluation in order to provide both formative and summative insights for the BHP Foundation, Program partners, and education stakeholders more broadly about the role that networks play in partners' work. The development of purposeful networks of collaboration is a key component of both the Program-level theory of change and most of the individual partners' strategies. In this chapter, we discuss the first network case study we implemented, which focuses on UNW's work in Mexico. This case study serves as an example of our approach; we expect to conduct similar work with other interested partners during the remainder of the evaluation.

Our Approach to Network Analysis

Over the course of our evaluation, we will use a combination of qualitative and quantitative network analytic approaches to understand how evidence-based practices are shared within the educational context. These analyses focus primarily on process-based network case studies chosen in collaboration with several of the Program-funded partners. The network case studies will vary in focus but may include assessments of collaboration among people or organizations, the movement of innovations through a network, the use of network visualizations, and the use of network indexes and statistical approaches that help us understand these processes.

To conduct network case studies, we will rely on the following six types of data:

1. qualitative interview data from the BHP Foundation, its Program-funded partners, and strategic network partners
2. information about the entities involved in these networks
3. brief questionnaires about collaborations administered to the Program-funded partners
4. visualizations based on aggregated responses to questionnaires
5. network statistics created from the network data
6. iterative presentation, discussion, and collaborative interpretation of the network diagrams.

Drawing on what we learn from our evaluation of these processes, we will make network-based recommendations for maximizing collaboration and the spread and adoption of evidence-based practices within the global education community (Valente, 2012; Valente et al., 2015).

Case Example: Networks Supporting UN Women's Second Chance Education Work in Mexico

For this initial report, we worked with UNW's Mexico country office to explore the organizations involved in its Second Chance Education Programme around the country. There are four stated goals for Second Chance Education Programme activities. They are delivering second chance education content, increasing employment and entrepreneurship as a result of second chance education, improving social norms associated with second chance education activities and target populations through advocacy, and changing policy at the national and regional levels. On the basis of the understanding that certain network structures are more effective for specific activities, we collaboratively explored with UNW Mexico how the structure of context-specific networks corresponds to the desired outcomes and activities for the key goals. The data collected and the resulting diagrams can be used to think strategically about network growth, building and maintaining important relationships, and increasing network resilience to shocks.

Reading the Network Diagrams

For demonstration purposes, we focus attention on three diagrams, corresponding to three of the four key stated goals of the UNW project in Mexico: second chance education delivered, social norms improved, and policy changes enacted.[1]

[1] The fourth diagram, corresponding to impacts on employment and entrepreneurship, was similar in structure and interpretation to the diagram for delivery of second chance education; therefore, we do not include it here

A limitation of this analysis is that findings may have gaps or be biased by having input only from the UNW team and its three key implementing partners as opposed to from everyone in the network. We intentionally made this trade-off to reduce data collection burden on partners.

Visualizing the Delivery of Second Chance Education in Mexico

Figure 5.1 visualizes the organizations—both government (triangles) and nongovernmental (circles)—that are collaborating with each other and with UNW to deliver second chance education in Mexico. The organizations we surveyed to gather this data—UNW and three key implementation partners that it relied on to expand the reach of its programs, one from each region where second chance education operates in Mexico—are represented as squares. More-connected nodes are placed in the center, nodes that are connected to each other are placed near each other, and nodes with similar patterns of connections are placed near each other.

From this diagram and our interviews with UNW representatives, we note the following takeaways:

- Most of the reported collaboration is clustered within (rather than across) geographic regions where the program is active, as shown by the separate clusters of connected red, green, and purple nodes. In other words, there is relatively little cross-region collaboration. Further examining collaboration across regions could help in understanding which types of organizations are key to the overall success and sustainability of second chance education delivery as a nationwide project. Note that yellow-node partners are listed as active in all regions of the country based on the type of work that they do, even if they have not reported collaboration with other listed partner organizations in every region.
- In the center (circled) is a core group of providers of second chance education content that collaborate with numerous organizations from all three regions. These content providers—commissioned by UNW—are holding together this network of geographically separated organizations.
- Although this network has three central actors (the content providers), there are also many connections among other organizations within each region. Each of the central content creators supports different organizations based on those organizations' interests. The receiving organizations further adapt and share materials to support the delivery of second chance education in each region.
- Among UNW's three key implementing partners (squares), the one in the Jalisco (green) region is more central and has more connections. This suggests that it has

in the interest of brevity. We note that the point we make about the higher capacity for partnership building of the key implementing partner in the Jalisco region is more pronounced in the context of employment and entrepreneurship, which UNW attributes in part to the combination of a stronger economy and lower prevalence of violence in Jalisco.

Figure 5.1
Delivery of Second Chance Education in Mexico

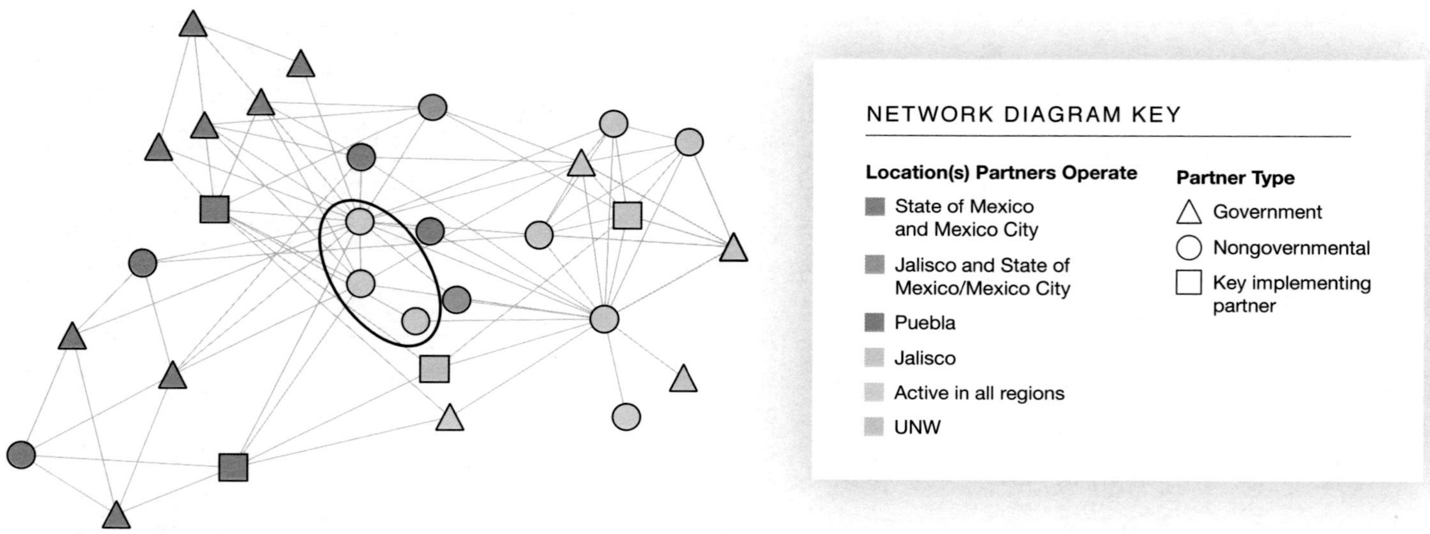

NOTE: UNW collaborates with all of the organizations in each diagram, but to avoid oversaturating the image, we show connections between the UNW node and other nodes only when UNW reported substantial collaboration with the organization around the goal in question.

higher capacity to build partnerships and support the delivery of services regionally than the other key implementing partners. UNW's representatives expressed interest in supporting the key implementing partners in the other two regions to reach a similar level of connectedness to help enhance the sustainability of the program in those regions. The representatives noted that involving the key implementing partners in the process of collecting data to inform the network analysis had an immediate impact by making those partners more aware and interested in focusing on partnership building.

Finally, we note that this diagram shows just one example of the delivery of second chance education. Each delivery model has its advantages and disadvantages. In the broader context of UNW's global second chance education work, UNW representatives described this Mexico model and its reliance on regional partners as potentially yielding a closer-knit network and a more sustainable program—albeit one that initially operates at a smaller scale—than models in other countries where delivery is mediated solely through the central government or a single implementing partner.

Collaboration Among Organizations Connected to UN Women

Our second diagram (Figure 5.2) shows reported collaboration among organizations in efforts led by UNW to change norms and attitudes around masculinity and female empowerment.

From this diagram of networks of collaborations for advocacy to change norms in Mexico, we note the following takeaways:

- A single central stakeholder organization is key to the campaign, providing and distributing campaign information and responding to feedback from its partners.
- In each region, locally connected organizations work to further refine and expand the reach of this campaign.
- This is the least densely connected of the network diagrams. Not all organizations might see changing norms as related to their own organizational missions. These activities might also be primarily regional and occur naturally and therefore are less often observed by or mentioned to UNW and key implementing partners as explicit areas of collaboration.
- This kind of hub-and-spoke structure tends to be effective for networks in which information gathering and dissemination occur (Semitiel-Garcia and Noguera-Mendez, 2012; Mostafa, 2020), as would be expected if content associated with changing norms is being collected or aggregated and then distributed back along the same lines of communication. According to discussions with UNW staff, this is the mechanism of action for the organizations engaged in this campaign.
- Because this network is so sparsely connected, if certain regional organizations leave, some organizations could become disconnected from the central stake-

Figure 5.2
Advocacy to Change Norms and Attitudes

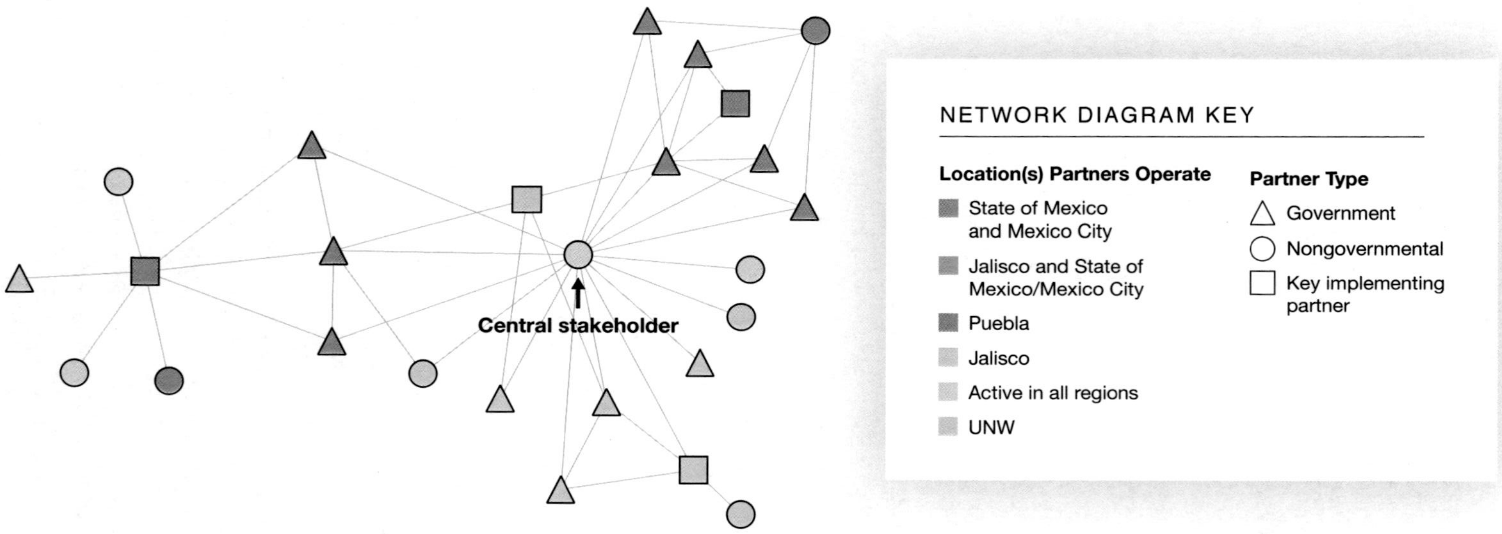

NOTE: UNW collaborates with all of the organizations in each diagram, but to avoid oversaturating the image, we show connections between the UNW node and other nodes only when UNW reported substantial collaboration with the organization around the goal in question.

holder organization. UNW could work to create more redundancy for organizational interactions in key areas to ensure that the network is resilient to organizational turnover and loss of organizational partners over time.

Facilitating Policy Change

The third network diagram (Figure 5.3) visualizes the interactions among organizations collaborating with UNW to influence policy in Mexico.

We found the following key takeaways from this diagram:

- Again, there is a clear regional clustering to the collaboration.
- In contrast to the previous diagrams, most of the collaboration in this network is highly centralized. There are three core stakeholders (the yellow cross-region actors clustered in the center). These are the federal labor and education ministries and Mexico's largest business council, which interact extensively with a surrounding ring of organizations.
- The organizations in the outer ring interact far less frequently with each other, however. This includes the key implementing partners, which—despite their capacity to build partnerships in the context of delivering second chance education—have drawn only modestly on that capacity to foster within- or cross-region connections to facilitate policy change.
- This core/periphery structure is often effective for networks that policymakers are using to gather information from a constituency to support decisionmaking at a higher level (Csemely et al., 2013; LaPira, Thomas, and Baumgartner, 2014). Within the core/periphery structure is a certain amount of hierarchy, as policy decisions are made centrally by the government or national-scale organizations.
- UNW might explore whether it would be useful to build relationships with policy stakeholder partners across regions or with regional representatives of the national organizations. These connections could be brokered either by UNW directly or via the key implementing partners. This could foster a sense of broader inclusion and engagement and build the capacity of those regional leaders to facilitate policy change locally. Cross-regional collaborations—rare in this network—could potentially facilitate policy change in addition.

Summary and Next Steps

Taken together, these network diagrams provide insight into the networks that support the goals of the UNW Second Chance Education Programme and shed light on the degree to which UNW's pilot of its program in Mexico is laying the groundwork for scaling up and sustaining that program. Possibly the clearest observation from our analyses is that the different goals lead to or rely upon different network structures. It

Figure 5.3
Facilitating Policy Change

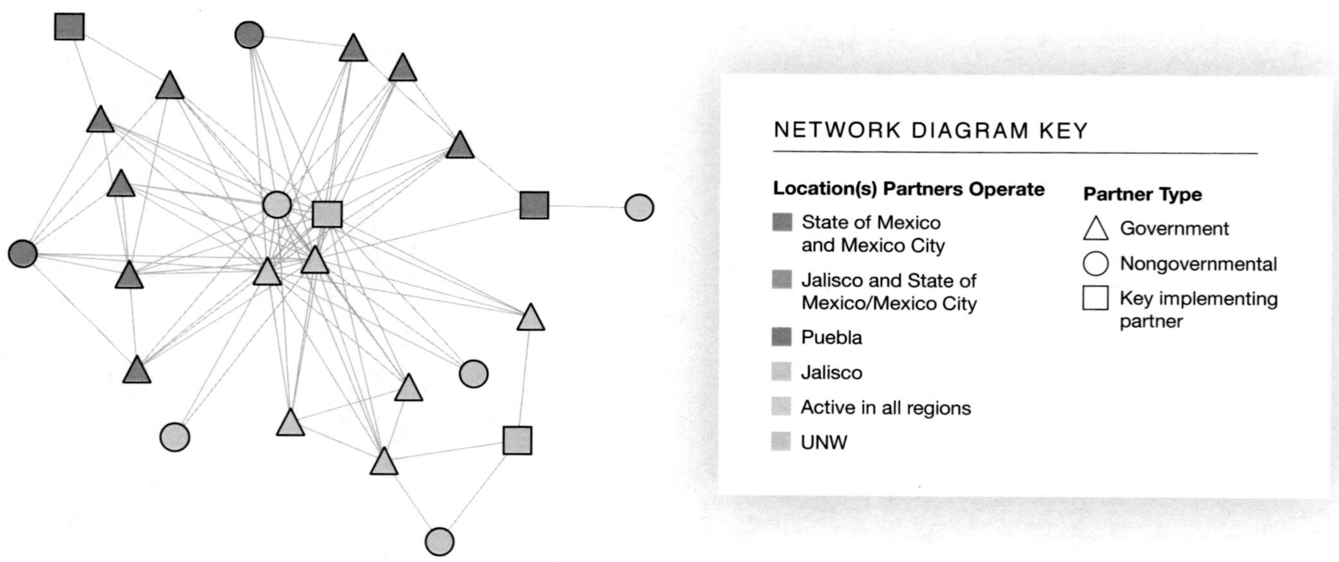

NOTE: UNW collaborates with all of the organizations in each diagram, but to avoid oversaturating the image, we show connections between the UNW node and other nodes only when UNW reported substantial collaboration with the organization around the goal in question.

is also clear that the work in Mexico involves a high degree of geographic regionalism. Depending on UNW's strategy and future goals, it might be useful to bring similar types of organizations together to encourage collaboration across regions. It might also be a good strategy to invest in capacity building that could help selected organizations become more connected regional leaders and, possibly, take on some national-level coordinating activities. Such capacity-building efforts could make the networks that UNW is fostering in Mexico more resilient and enable UNW itself to begin to step back from a direct coordinating role.

Going forward, we expect that exploration of other partners' networks will provide additional insight into the types of local and global networks that facilitate the different types of evidence-to-practice work they are engaged in. For example, we have begun to work with EEF to visualize the connections that it has fostered among its global network of organizations and individuals engaged in evidence dissemination to inform decisionmaking. We also plan to illustrate the development of CUE's network to support Scaling Lab innovations in Tanzania, as well as the development of CUE's global communities of practice that connect stakeholders across multiple Scaling Labs worldwide. We are working with TFA to illustrate, in one regional context, the pathways through which the direct contributions of its Community Impact Lab influence a larger group of key organizations through an informal alumni network.

In addition, for both the UNW case and other cases, we will explore how collaboration networks evolve and develop over time in tandem with the successes or challenges reported by the partner representatives. Through this work, we hope to better understand which types of networks contribute to the different core activities funded by the Program and how each of the partners has worked to develop more-sustainable and more-effective networks over time. We also hope that these exploratory analyses provide useful formative feedback throughout the course of our evaluation, providing a system-level view that allow decisions to be made based on entire networks rather than just one relationship at a time.

CHAPTER SIX

Strategic Approaches of Comparator Organizations

Strategies, interventions, and evaluation approaches used by other comparable organizations (which we call *comparators*) provide insights to inform the BHP Foundation's own strategic planning, enabling a better understanding of the factors that contribute to an effective global educational program. In this chapter, we analyze six efforts, each of which has some similarities or overlap with the work of the Program. We selected comparators from various organizations. These include corporate foundations working within the education investment landscape, other education-focused nongovernmental organizations, foundations focusing on evidence-to-practice initiatives in other fields (such as health), and wider social investment initiatives or research programs that share the BHP Foundation's evidence-to-practice goals. By examining the approaches of different types of organizations, we aim to provide a richer and more varied set of comparisons than would be derived from focusing on educational organizations alone.

Our case studies are focused on understanding the strategies, implementation activities, evaluation mechanisms, and achievements of each comparator. We then analyzed cross-cutting themes and commonalities. Research for the comparator case studies relied on two methods: desk research and interviews. Desk research involved documents produced by the comparator organization, including strategy documents, reports (including annual reports), evaluations, evaluation frameworks, and broader website material. Interviews were conducted with staff from each organization and were focused on individuals with direct involvement in the comparator's strategic planning, program implementation, or evaluation. Our interviews had a semistructured approach; questions followed a common template but were also tailored to the specifics of the comparator.

Overview of the Cases

The six case studies used for this analysis are outlined in Table 6.1. Three are focused primarily on education, two have a cross-sector focus, and one is focused on health. Five of the six comparators focus on low- and middle-income countries, while the BHP Foundation has a comparatively stronger focus on underrepresented and marginalized communities. We do not have precise data on the scale of each comparator's efforts,

Table 6.1
Key Features of the Comparators

Comparator	Type of Organization	Sectoral Focus	Mission	Geographic Focus
Gates Global Education Program (Gates Foundation)	Private foundation	Education	Improving foundational learning and tackling the "learning crisis" (Gates Foundation, undated-c)	Focus on India and sub-Saharan African countries
Mastercard Foundation	Private foundation	Education and financial inclusion	To "advance education and financial inclusion to catalyze prosperity in developing countries" (Mastercard Foundation, undated-a)	African countries
Education Development Center (EDC)	Global nonprofit organization	Education	To design, implement, and evaluate programs "to improve education, health, and economic opportunity worldwide" (EDC, undated-a)	Global (United States and 22 countries around the world)
Abdul Latif Jameel Poverty Action Lab (J-PAL)	Global research center	Cross-sectoral (including education, public health, agriculture, and microfinance)	To "reduce global poverty by ensuring that policy is informed by scientific evidence" (J-PAL, undated-a)	Global (with focus on low-income countries)
The European and Developing Countries Clinical Trials Partnership (EDCTP)	Public-private partnership	Health	To support "high-quality collaborative research to accelerate the development of new or improved medical interventions" (EDCTP, undated-a)	Sub-Saharan African countries
The Alliance for Useful Evidence (Alliance)	Public-private partnership	Cross-sectoral (education, health, policing, and social care)	To promote "the smarter use of evidence in social policy and practice" (Alliance, undated)	United Kingdom

but based on public records we believe that most have portfolios of activity and investments significantly larger than the Program; only the Alliance appears to have a substantially smaller-scale funding footprint.

In the following section, we describe several cross-cutting themes that we identified about the six comparators' strategies and how they operate. In some cases, these themes show contrasts with the BHP Foundation's approach; in others, there is significant overlap in how the comparators approach their work.

Cross-Cutting Themes Related to Strategies and Implementation

Clear Strategic Vision

The comparators that are funder organizations emphasized the importance of having a clear strategic vision and plan for their investments, which they articulated in different ways (Table 6.2). Similar to the Program, some developed an explicit theory of change or logic model delineating how their activities and interim outcomes will contribute toward longer-term systemic outcomes (and in some cases broader impacts) associated with their strategic goals. For example, the Bill & Melinda Gates Foundation (Gates Foundation), EDCTP, and the Alliance have all developed their own theories of change (Alliance, 2018; EDCTP, 2019; Gates Foundation, undated-a). The Mastercard Foundation adopted a strategic plan for 2018–2030, which details priority areas seen as essential to achieving a specific ambitious impact goal. J-PAL has adopted a broad framework, referred to as Pathways to Policy Change, that conceptualizes the contributions of the center's global strategy for maximizing evidence use in policymaking (J-PAL, undated-b). Regional J-PAL offices have the flexibility to determine their own local theories of change.

Comparators' strategies vary in how specific and directive they are. Organizations coordinating investments toward a single impact target tend to be more directive, focusing on the interdependence of different work strands toward that goal. Others, more similar to the BHP Foundation, articulate broader common principles or theories that connect wide-ranging investments.

Working in Partnership

Across all the case studies, comparators seek to build partnerships between themselves and other organizations to maximize their impact, whether as funders or as intervention partners. Because of the mature and well-established nature of the field, organizations operating within the education space particularly emphasize partnerships. In a

Table 6.2
Elements of Comparators' Strategic Visions

Rely on Theory of Change	Rely on Strategic Plans	Rely on Broad Program-Level Strategy with Regional/Project-Level Theories of Change
The Gates Foundation's theory of action relates its work in public goods, data and accountability, and advocacy to outputs contributing to strategic goals.	The Mastercard Foundation's strategic plan (2018–2030) outlines key activities to reach goals and guiding principles.	J-PAL's framework outlines six overlapping conceptual pathways for creating policy change. J-PAL regional offices have their own theories of change.
EDCTP's program intervention logic identifies three pathways to impact: clinical research, capacity development, and coordination and partnerships. Outputs, outcomes, and impacts are delineated for each pathway.	EDCTP has developed a Strategic Business Plan for 2014–2024, which sets out five key objectives for the EDCTP program, with associated targets and outcomes for each.	Although EDC does not have an organization-wide theory of change or strategic plan, individual EDC projects have their own theories of change.
The Alliance's theory of change relates to smarter evidence use for behavior change, on the basis of three conditions—capability, opportunity, and motivation.		

crowded landscape, working with partners—whether with one or two key partners or as part of a broader network—could help reduce duplication and ensure that an organization's work builds on others' knowledge and experience (Edwards, 2018).

We found two broad models of partnership in our analysis. The first model is building a close relationship with a key partner and leveraging its work. J-PAL has built a number of close partnerships with other organizations, including with Pratham, an Indian nongovernmental organization with which J-PAL has collaborated for more than 20 years. The Gates Foundation has followed a similar model, hoping to support major preexisting organizations, such as the World Bank, which, according to interviewees, has provided the Gates Foundation with a "framework and vision for what they wanted to do" as an organization.

In the second model, an organization focuses on building a broad network of organizations with similar goals. The Alliance emphasizes partnership with a wide range of other organizations, including government bodies, civil society organizations, and academia (Mthiyane, 2018). The Mastercard Foundation was a founding member of the Partnership to Strengthen Innovation and Practice in Secondary Education (PSIPSE), a collaborative donor network that existed from 2011 to 2019 (PSIPSE, undated). EDCTP is a medical research funding partnership between countries in Europe and sub-Saharan Africa.[1] Additional examples of these two models of partnership outlined above are highlighted below in Table 6.3.

For both J-PAL and the Gates Foundation, partners tend to be implementation experts and play a key role in conveying shared ideas and frameworks into practice. For organizations engaging in a network, fellow donors tend to be crucial, and this is most clearly illustrated by the cases of the Mastercard Foundation and EDCTP. The full range of partner types is displayed in Figure 6.1.

As a relative newcomer to the field, the BHP Foundation has partnered mostly with organizations that are well established and capable of independently contributing to the global education reform movement. Relative to the comparators, the Program

Table 6.3
Approach to Partnerships

Close Key Partner Relationships	Networks of Multiple Organizations
• J-PAL partners with Pratham in "Teaching at the Right Level" (TaRL) in Zambia. • The Gates Foundation is now working with the World Bank to develop the Global Education Policy Dashboard. The World Bank is identified as a key partner in the Gates Foundation's theory of action.	• The Alliance stresses collaboration with a wide variety of partners in its theory of change. • The Mastercard Foundation collaborates in a secondary education network. They issue shared requests for proposals, enabling grantees to propose project ideas to multiple donors. • EDCTP fosters collaboration among member states, between European donors and African researchers, and among African research organizations.

[1] The aim of these partnerships is to "increase the likelihood that new evidence generated by EDCTP-funded studies feeds into national and international policy and practice" (EDCTP, 2018, p. 10).

Figure 6.1
Types of Partners

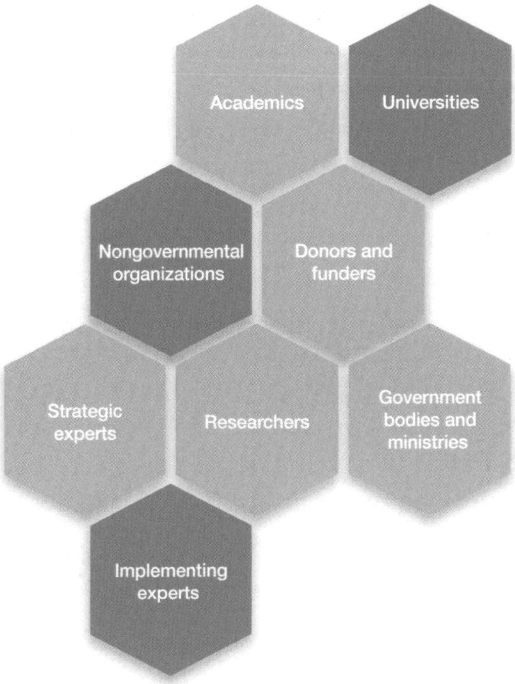

appears more independent, with less formal coordination with other organizations supporting complementary work. The Program also differs from some other comparators in not targeting a specific geographic area. This limits the need for local implementing partners but also potentially limits the capacity to drive systemic change in a local context.

Adapting to Local Contexts

Adapting to local contexts is a vital step for those organizations most involved in scaling up programs and interventions across borders. For example, when EDC sought to extend its Work Ready Now curriculum to Rwanda, a key part of its work was to engage closely with local stakeholders to understand their needs and priorities and adapt the program as needed. A similar process took place in J-PAL's scale-up of TaRL, which was initially developed in India with Pratham. It conceived of the Catch Up program, which has since been piloted and extended across the country. Both EDC and J-PAL have set up local spin-off organizations (Akazi Kanoze Access and TaRL Africa, respectively), which are staffed by local experts.

Building Local Capacities and Networks

All comparators emphasize the need to build local capacities. Here, comparators stress the need to provide local organizations and individuals with the longer-term infrastructure, resources, skills, and expertise to be able to plan, implement, evaluate, and scale up interventions themselves. This is consistent with the strategies and foci of the BHP Foundation's funded partners. According to one interviewee at EDC, capacity building forms a key part of all the organization's work.[2] The Mastercard Foundation has also supported grantees during the preparation, implementation, and evaluation of programs, and by working with education ministries to support system-level improvements in national education systems. EDCTP issues annual requests for proposals for capacity-building projects.[3]

Comparators have also supported local monitoring, evaluation, and learning capabilities, as discussed in later sections. Figure 6.2 provides an overview of the different types of capacity building undertaken by comparators. Figure 6.3 shows the range of local stakeholders targeted by comparators' capacity-building efforts.

According to EDCTP, the aim of this capacity-building work is to create an "enabling environment" for research (EDCTP, 2018). For the Mastercard Foundation, the enabling environment is both a goal of its capacity-building efforts and a criterion for selecting focus countries. Under its new Young Africa Works strategy, the Mastercard Foundation focuses its attention on implementing its interventions in countries that already possess an "enabling environment for growth, job creation and skills development" (Mastercard Foundation, undated-b). Factors considered include a country's policy and strategy, the existence of a thriving business sector, levels of innovation within the digital economy, and key population demographics (Mastercard Foundation, 2019).

In line with the BHP Foundation's own focus, several comparators also work to support the development of local networks. Strengthening networks within a local context could deliver numerous benefits, including support for the scale-up of interventions, shared learning, and common platforms for advocacy and fundraising.

One way to support networks is through funding. EDCTP, for example, has used networking grants to support collaboration and cooperation among African organizations. Another way to support networks is through convening. EDCTP, Mastercard Foundation, EDC, and the Alliance have all used convening approaches to establish connections and alliances between local organizations, providing opportunities for development of networks at both the organizational and the individual level. Ways in

---

2 In the context of its Akazi Kanoze program, EDC supported the training of almost 600 local trainers to deliver the program, while also helping to build the organizational capacity of 63 nongovernmental organizations and ministries to run and administer it (EDC, undated-b).

3 Projects supported include infrastructure and clinical facility development; training and mentorships; and support to governments to strengthen their ethical, regulatory, and legal frameworks surrounding medical research (EDCTP, 2018, p. 19).

Figure 6.2
Types of Capacity-Building Activities

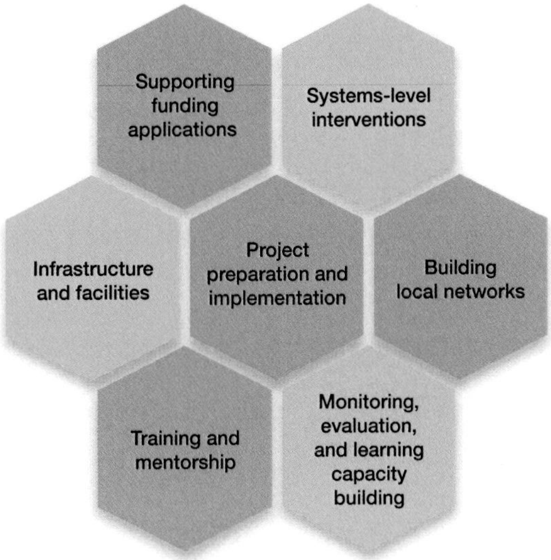

Figure 6.3
Local Stakeholders Targeted by Capacity-Building Efforts

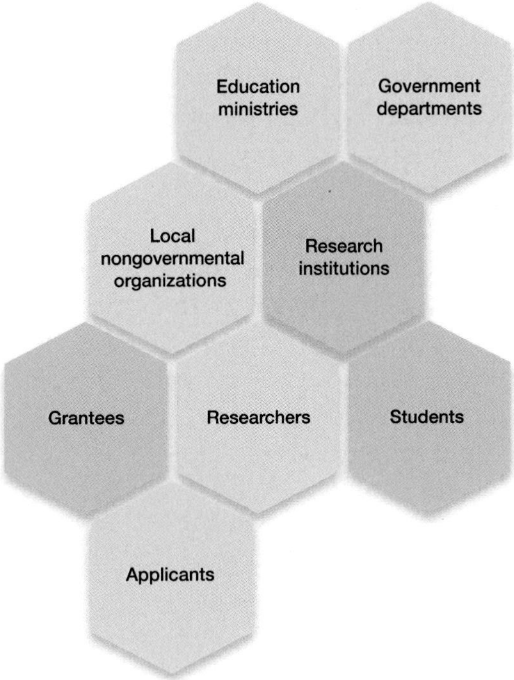

Table 6.4
Ways in Which Comparators Build Local Partnerships

Funding	Convenings
• EDCTP's networking grants fund four regional Networks of Excellence in Africa, which include research institutions that share resources, multisite clinical trials research, cross-organizational capacity building, and advocacy for political and financial support.	• The Mastercard Foundation convened local grantees and secondary education stakeholders and experts through in-country events. • EDC used convening to establish connections between local organizations, nongovernmental organizations, labor ministries, and the private sector. • EDCTP's biennial forum connects scientists in Europe and Africa. • The Alliance uses convenings to develop organizational networks and its network of individual Evidence Champions.

which comparators have used funding and convening to support local networks are further detailed in Table 6.4.

Ensuring Cost-Effectiveness

For a number of comparator organizations, keeping cost as a central consideration throughout projects represents an important means of promoting sustainability. At the end of its scaled-up Akazi Kanoze 2 project, EDC provided the Rwandan government with budgetary information and a cost analysis of what it would take to continue to run the trainings in schools (Cyr, 2017). J-PAL aims to streamline interventions and make monitoring and evaluation as cost-effective as possible. Interviewees have said that cost of the Global Education Policy Dashboard that the Gates Foundation is developing with the World Bank has been carefully considered as "front and center of the design and implementation process." The Gates Foundation and the World Bank have used streamlined, cheaper versions of preexisting, open-source instruments, such as the Service Delivery Indicators initiative and SABER, so that countries can freely use and integrate them into their own monitoring systems.

Overall, attention to cost-effectiveness is particularly relevant for programs engaged in scaling up established interventions (as opposed to pilots). The BHP Foundation's strategy and most of its funded partners are focused on novel innovations and put less emphasis on measuring cost-effectiveness. However, considering cost-effectiveness could also be valuable early in project life cycles to determine whether there is a feasible pathway to sustainable impact in the long run. Figure 6.4 depicts some ways of ensuring cost-effectiveness.

Developing Public Goods

As with the Program, comparator organizations have sought to develop public goods in education (see Table 6.5). This is an explicit part of the Gates Foundation's strategy; its dashboard is a comprehensive information source that aims to show policymakers

Figure 6.4
Ways of Ensuring Cost-Effectiveness

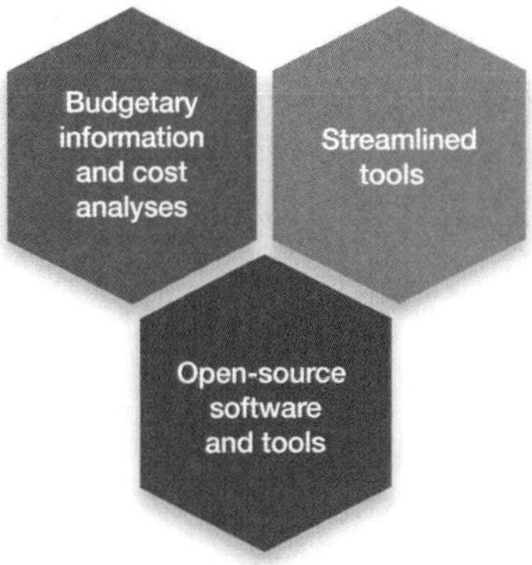

around the world what are the key drivers of and the key barriers to learning in their countries (World Bank, 2019c). External interviewees have said that the Gates Foundation's strategic commitment to public goods is a highly valuable and unusual asset in the global education space.

Other organizations have also developed freely available resources. J-PAL, through years of conducting RCTs in education, has contributed greatly to the global evidence base and provided policymakers around the world with a better understanding of what makes for effective learning. Similarly, EDC has developed curricula, such as Work Ready Now and Read Right Now (EDC, undated-b and undated-c), which have been implemented and adapted in different countries across the world. Policymakers benefit from such efforts, and both J-PAL and EDC also develop public goods for local, on-the-ground users. Both Teaching at the Right Level and Akazi Kanoze, respectively, have developed curricula and teaching strategies that are free to use by teachers and instructors worldwide.

Table 6.5
Types of Public Good and Key Audiences

Public Good	Audience	Comparator
High-quality data and monitoring, evaluation, and learning tools	Global policymakers and government officials	Gates Foundation
Evidence and proof of concepts	International development organizations, researchers, and global policymaker	J-PAL; EDC
Educational resources and curricula	Local teachers and instructors	J-PAL; EDC

Diversity of Evaluation Approaches

The BHP Foundation is not alone in the challenge it faces in evaluating broad, future, and sometimes qualitative impacts. We found a diversity of approaches in the way different comparators evaluate their work, as shown in Table 6.6. Some have mature, comprehensive approaches to evaluation, while others have emerging processes, in part reflecting the challenges of assessing the outcomes of these types of programs.

We also observe variation in how evaluations are conducted, with some conducting all evaluation work in-house and others bringing in external evaluators to support evaluation work (Table 6.7). There are different models for the use of external evaluation support. In some cases, evaluators are brought in to conduct a discrete, one-off evaluation, using an independent and external perspective. Others develop a longer-term partnership with an evaluation or learning partner to provide ongoing support with monitoring and evaluation efforts. In all cases, however, some evaluation work—particularly monitoring of process indicators—is done in-house alongside that external support.

A wide range of approaches are used to evaluate the performance of organizations' investments. These include process measures, target-based assessment, desk research, surveys, publication tracking, interview measures, and RCTs. This variety corresponds to the diversity, complexity, and the challenges inherent to measuring many of the comparators' contributions. However, evaluation activity might be seen as not only a process for internal learning and adaptation but also an investment in a public good and a means of generating insights that can inform global priorities. Examples of different evaluation practices from the comparator organizations are provided in Table 6.8.

All the comparators use process measures, which are typically focused on operational aspects of the work, to assess their performance to at least some degree. These measures identify activities that those organizations are conducting and assess how well they are performing—usually covering aspects of effectiveness and efficiency—in delivering those activities.

Comparator organizations acknowledge that measuring outcomes from interventions in education is not straightforward. Interestingly, the Gates Foundation has

Table 6.6
Diversity of Evaluation Approaches

Mature, Comprehensive Evaluation Approach	Less Mature, Emerging Evaluation Processes
• EDCTP has a comprehensive program of monitoring and evaluation mechanisms, including indicators, externally conducted impact evaluations, and cases of EDCTP-sponsored projects. • The Mastercard Foundation has an internal monitoring and evaluation team and adopted an impact strategy outlining its approach to impact measurement.	• The Alliance acknowledges that evaluation is not one of its strengths; it has some assessment of progress, which is largely process-oriented. • The Gates Foundation's approach is largely internally led and process-oriented.

Table 6.7
Use of In-House and External Evaluation Capacity

How Evaluation Is Conducted	Approach
Evaluation conducted in-house	EDC conducts evaluations through a specialist in-house evaluation team
In-house evaluation supplemented by discrete external evaluations	EDCTP conducts evaluations in-house, including monitoring against indicators and case studies. It also commissions external independent impact evaluations.
In-house capacity supported by long-term partnership with external evaluators	The Mastercard Foundation has an internal monitoring and evaluation team, supplemented with an external long-term learning partner, Mathematica. It conducts thematic evaluations and also evaluation support and guidance to award holders.

Table 6.8
Examples of Evaluation Approaches

Approach	Examples
Process measures	• EDCTP has a set of indicators about operational performance, such as the processing of grant applications, organization of stakeholder meetings, and levels of participation of states (EDCTP, 2019). • The Alliance measures progress of activities against targets, such as producing six publications over three years, appointing 20 Evidence Champions, increasing its network by 50 percent, and developing six new strategic relationships (Mthiyane and Breckon, 2020).
Mixed-methods assessment of outcomes	• The Mastercard Foundation worked with its learning partner, Mathematica, to conduct evaluations relying on qualitative approaches, such as interviews with grantees and other stakeholders. • EDCTP's evaluations, conducted by external evaluators, draw on indicators, desk research, surveys, and interviews. • The Alliance conducts surveys about training courses, conducts interviews about Evidence Champions, and analyzes such publication metrics as downloads per publication. • EDC prioritizes assessing capacity building through interviews with program graduates and metrics, such as the number of businesses created and employment rates (Mthiyane and Breckon, 2020).
RCTs	• EDC uses RCTs infrequently but acknowledges their value. EDC staff highlight the cost and administrative burden of RCTs and their limitations for scale-up and scale-out of interventions. • The Gates Foundation uses RCTs in some cases, but staff note concerns about their external validity and challenges in implementing RCT findings. • J-PAL is a global leader in the use of RCTs. Staff acknowledge challenges with RCTs, particularly the need to go beyond the RCT evidence to understand how to enable an intervention to be used in new contexts.

stated publicly that "program teams are not expected to use evaluation to sum up the results of foundation strategies," noting that the impact of its investments "cannot be easily differentiated from [its] partners" (Gates Foundation, undated-b). Organizations adopt a range of approaches to address this issue, most commonly using qualitative or mixed-methods approaches to evaluation. Some organizations take a more ad-hoc approach, tailoring evaluation methods to different aspects of their work or focusing on key organizational aims.

One approach that can help assess the effectiveness of specific interventions is the RCT, which can provide high-quality evidence on whether well-defined interventions deliver benefits. However, views on RCTs and their relevance were mixed across comparator organizations. Some use them relatively infrequently but note their importance in specific contexts as the gold standard in demonstrating the effectiveness of an intervention. J-PAL, in particular, is noted for its use of RCTs and valuing them not only for confirming the efficacy of specific interventions but for testing mechanisms of impact that may be generalizable. However, all of the comparators acknowledge the challenges and limitations of RCTs, including cost, administrative burden, and inapplicability for some types of interventions. Comparator views reflect the wider discussion in the literature regarding the value of RCTs, coupled with the acknowledgment that they are not a panacea and need to be considered as part of a wider toolkit of evaluation tools and techniques (Bamberger, Rao, and Woodcock, 2010; Barrett and Carter, 2010; Pieterse, 2020).

It is also worth noting that evaluations can be conducted at different levels of aggregation, as shown in Table 6.9. Organizations can conduct a cross-cutting evaluation at the portfolio level or can monitor and evaluate at lower levels of aggregation within their portfolios. An award-level evaluation is often specified as a requirement of funding for awardees—and might apply to some organizations as award holders themselves. Evaluations sometimes cluster awards and activities in different ways—thematically, by program, or by country.

Table 6.9
Levels of Aggregation in Evaluation

Award-Level Evaluation	Cross-Cutting Evaluations	Whole Portfolio Evaluation
• EDC receives funding from donors, such as the U.S. Agency for International Development, which requires key indicators at project inception. • The Mastercard Foundation requires its award holders to use monitoring data and encouraged grantees to evaluate their own projects, with capacity support provided.	• Through a partner, the Mastercard Foundation conducts evaluations of its portfolios of investments. The Mastercard Foundation uses mixed-methods approaches in output-focused evaluations at the program, country, and mission levels.	• All comparators collect process measures, which typically span the whole portfolio. • EDCTP has periodic evaluations from external evaluators, covering the whole portfolio, using a quantitative and qualitative mixed-methods approach.

Summary and Reflections for the BHP Foundation

Reflecting on the observations across this set of case studies, we identify a number of key lessons and areas for the BHP Foundation to consider further in the development of its program of work. We also note areas of similarity and distinctiveness for the Program in comparison with the other organizations we examined.

First, we note the benefits of a clear strategic vision and direction. There are many possible visions, but providing clarity of focus and a road map for how to reach this vision has proved valuable across many of these organizations. Within that road map, partnership is likely to play an important role, given the maturity of the field and the number of actors already working in this space. Partnership can follow different models—for example, a close relationship leveraging the existing infrastructure of a key implementing partner, targeted collaborations with peer funders, or membership in a broad network with shared goals. Alongside this, local partnerships and engagements are likely to assist with the delivery and success of educational interventions, including by ensuring those interventions are adapted to local contexts.

Capacity building and network building on the local level are important for many comparator organizations and, alongside considerations of affordability, represent key factors needed to support the sustainability of new interventions beyond a single project. This local capacity, referred to as an *enabling environment*, might include evaluation capacity, the capacity to adopt new ideas, and the ability use evidence within the wider policy landscape.

Learning is also important at the organizational and sector levels, with several of the comparator examples highlighting the importance of and challenges in effectively sharing learning both within and across organizations internationally. We highlight the importance of adaptive strategies, effective communication, and the need to formalize learning as accessible and wider shared public goods to ensure efficient learning and use of evidence across organizations.

Evaluation of educational interventions beyond commonly used process measures is challenging and likely requires a mix of approaches. RCTs can contribute to the evaluation of interventions, but they do not work in all contexts or provide all the evidence needed for scale-up and translation of learning. Qualitative evidence also plays an important role in program evaluation. Approaches to evaluation need not be uniform across the Program, and rigorous impact analyses related to specific outcomes or projects can add value and help spur broader investment.

Overall, the BHP Foundation has many areas of alignment with other organizations engaged in evidence-to-practice work, including an appreciation of the importance of identifying key implementation partners, building local capacity, and paying attention to enabling environments. As newcomers to the field, the BHP Foundation has sought to strategically identify areas of underinvestment in which its investments have the potential to serve as a catalyst for potential step changes in education practice. As a consequence, it has invested in a wide range of mechanisms for translating evidence into practice rather than focusing narrowly on a particular region or issue within education. The BHP Foundation also seems to be unique in developing an explicit theory about translating evidence into practice as the main theme of its work regarding education and in investing in interventions up and down the decisionmaking pipeline. At the same time, some of the comparators have more-specific global or country-specific targets; over time, the BHP Foundation could consider how its investments can jointly contribute to systemic changes in specific contexts.

CHAPTER SEVEN

Conclusions and Recommendations

This report lays out our system for evaluating the BHP Foundation's Program and describes initial insights from our work. Over the coming five years, we will analyze insights from the elements described here: progress aligned with the theory of change, success in meeting goals articulated in the key indicators, ways in which Program partners develop and use their networks, and key trends and lessons learned with respect to notable challenges and areas of progress. Although it is still too early to determine what is or is not succeeding, we offer some thoughts about the way forward.

Specify Pathways to a Step Change in Global Education Practice

BHP Foundation leadership views success as making a significant contribution to a step change in education. Program partners are undertaking activities to produce near-term direct impacts on education; an important next step is further defining evidence to enhance confidence that investments are making a difference, informing decision-making practice and policy, and bettering educational outcomes.

The theory of change presented here illustrates how Program efforts could make indirect contributions to longer-term impacts on education beyond the funding period. In broad strokes, the BHP Foundation is experimenting with multiple possible ways of connecting evidence to practice, such as toolkits, scaling up good practice, investments in leaders and communities, and seed funding for pilot programs. We think there is an opportunity to be more specific about those pathways to success, which, in turn, might support progress in measurement and assist in selecting or giving guidance to new partners. A next step for our evaluation will be to work collaboratively with the BHP Foundation and Program partners to more clearly articulate the pathways to global impact and the assumptions underlying these pathways. This will include pathways at both the overarching level of the Program and at the level of each partner's contribution to the Program's overall success.

Identify Long-Term Outcome Indicators

The long-term outcomes toward which the Program seeks to contribute will take more than five years of partners' current BHP Foundation–funded work to fully realize, and indicators collected by the partners to track their own progress are currently not intended to measure whether the Program on the whole is having its intended long-term impact. In addition to more fully articulating the pathways through which its partners' work will yield long-term improvements in educational attainment and educational investments, the BHP Foundation should identify indicators that it will use to gauge progress along those pathways toward long-term outcomes. These indicators might include (but should not be limited to) those being collected as part of the partners' existing reporting and evaluation processes and additional indicators that partners would be able collect with additional time and resources. In particular, indicators should be trackable beyond the current span of the funded projects to understand the enduring impacts of the BHP Foundation's investments. This work would test key assumptions about how interim outcomes contribute to long-term outcomes. These indicators should pair quantitative targets and metrics, where feasible, to identify and collect case studies that illustrate the impacts of BHP Foundation–funded work.

Apply Solutions Simultaneously at a Systems Level in a Particular Geographic Area

The BHP Foundation is investing in multiple areas of the enabling environment for improving education in multiple geographic areas. The BHP Foundation seems to be unique among the comparator organizations in investing in interventions being carried out up and down the decisionmaking pipeline, running the gamut from governments to teachers to communities and business leaders. The BHP Foundation could consider how its investments can jointly or synergistically contribute to systemic changes or scale up evidence-based initiatives in one or more specific contexts. This could also help to address a common challenge faced by partners about implementation at local levels. Such investments could be made in collaboration with currently funded partners or could be a key consideration when identifying additional partners for future funded work.

Elevate Convening, Linking, and Facilitating as Part of the Foundation's Role

The BHP Foundation could better articulate its leadership role above and beyond its investment in particular partners, especially in terms of convening and linking stakeholders concerned with improving global education. The BHP Foundation might wish to further connect with the wider global education reform movement, both as collaborators and as audiences for key insights from the Program's work. This could include additional convening (for example, through a highly visible event), policy advocacy, collaboration with other funders on shared priorities, and advocating for and facilitating the work of the partners through the foundation's own networks. Multiple funded partners noted the usefulness of GBC-Ed, as well as other connections that the BHP Foundation had the ability to facilitate. One option is convening multiple types of national stakeholders about further implementation of evidence within an education system. Other options are coordinating with other funders about investing in complementary endeavors, convening to disseminate global public goods developed as part of the Program's investments, serving as a matchmaker among education organizations and other funders, and working with others to invest in amplifying successes identified through the Program's investments. Improving education relies on many types of actors, and convening, linking, and facilitating could help scale up successful approaches.

Focus on Specific Opportunities for Collaboration Among Partners

The Program partners already regard the BHP Foundation as a facilitator, connecting partners and serving as a thought leader. The BHP Foundation could further connect current and future partners in ways that lead to concrete collaborations that advance the collective impact of the Program. Partners noted that the BHP Foundation might facilitate events and opportunities that go beyond knowledge sharing and that connect partners to each other on particular issues (either within a particular country or worldwide). As the BHP Foundation has knowledge of each partner organization's work, it could envision and facilitate specific activities that particular partners could work on together locally or globally. This could also include helping to remove barriers to collaboration among partners, particularly at local levels; partners noted that, even in countries where they are working, they are often not working on the same issues in the same communities. Possible areas of collaboration suggested by partners include tools for assessing innovations and presenting evidence, techniques for scaling education interventions, and modeling return on investment for interventions.

Integrate Return on Investment in Some Future Projects

For programs at the pilot stage, return on investment may not be the most important consideration. Indeed, initial stages of new projects inherently involve risk and the opportunity for a wide range of potential returns, and the BHP Foundation's resources put it in a position to absorb such risk as part of a learning process. At the same time, as projects are selected to continue or as they enter new stages of maturity, the BHP Foundation could build consideration for increasing, sustaining, and measuring cost-effectiveness or return on investment into these projects, much as some other comparator organizations do. Cost-effectiveness estimates or estimates of social or financial return on investment could be integrated into partners' individual evaluations when their efforts are at an appropriate stage and when appropriate tools exist in the context of education.

Estimating returns on investment, particularly when targeted outcomes are varied and might take a long time to pay off, is a complex effort and requires articulation of key assumptions grounded in the best available evidence of long-term impacts. However, this work has several potential benefits. It can better communicate to diverse audiences the intended scale of long-term impacts and contributions of Program activities and help avoid a narrow focus on only those interim outcome measures that are convenient to measure. It could also increase clarity around intended pathways to impact and facilitate monitoring of key assumptions about necessary conditions for effectiveness and efficiency. Finally, as more funders and program implementers conduct these types of analyses of social or financial return on investment, the field's collective knowledge base for how best to estimate contributions is strengthened; this can facilitate more grounded, more accurate, and more comprehensive valuations of impact over time.

APPENDIX A

Key Indicator Tables

This appendix lists the key indicators that we identified from the BHP Foundation partners linked to the activities and interim outcomes of the Program-level theory of change. It also includes our baseline long-term outcome dashboard drawn from SDG4 indicators compiled from the World Bank for a set of ten countries where multiple BHP Foundation partners are engaged in significant project work.

For both the activities tables (A.1–A.5) and the interim outcomes tables (A.6–A.9), we list the partner from which the indicator was drawn, the indicator, the partner-provided target (if available), and the current status as documented in the partner's reporting (if available). We reiterate that the same indicator can measure progress toward one or more activities or one or more outcomes, but that each indicator is categorized as either an activity indicator or an interim outcome indicator. The tables include a column that lists the other activities or interim outcomes for which the indicator also serves as a measure of progress. The interim outcome indicator tables also list the activity or activities that result in the outcome being measured by the indicator in the tables.

Several points mentioned in Chapter Three should be reiterated. First, we recognize that each partner operates at a somewhat different place of that theory of change, conducting different sets of activities in pursuit of different objectives. There is no expectation that each partner have the same number of indicators for each activity or interim outcome as the other partners (or that they have any indicators at all). Just as the five projects themselves should be viewed as mutually reinforcing, so too should the indicators be understood in the collective. Progress on indicators in each of these buckets of activities or interim outcomes is an important signal that, collectively, the partners' work is having the results that the BHP Foundation views as important to laying the groundwork for longer-term impacts in line with its theory of change. However, it would be inappropriate to assess any *individual* partner's success using this framework.

The SDG long-term outcome dashboard table (Table A.10) is included to monitor the status of a select number of key indicators that are linked to the long-term outcomes that the BHP Foundation is pursuing through the Program. Given the numerous factors that affect these measures, as well as the time lag involved (i.e., the measures are not contemporaneous), the dashboard should be considered as suggestive and illustrative only. The BHP Foundation seeks to shift indicators such as these in the positive direction, but it is not possible to isolate the impacts of its Program from other contributors to trends. As described in Chapter Three, we propose linking these high-level indicators that provide contextual information on the countries in which the Program is particularly active with targeted measures designed to trace the contributions of the Program over the longer term.

Table A.1
Key Activity Indicators: Curate Evidence About Improving Education

Partner	Indicator	Also Indicator for Activities	Target	Status	Last Updated
CUE	Number of knowledge products (publications, tools, podcasts, etc.) developed by the Innovations team	Disseminate evidence	N/A	37 knowledge products	June 2020
CUE	Number of knowledge products (publications, tools, podcasts, etc.) developed by the Analyze Data team	Disseminate evidence	N/A	16 knowledge products	June 2020
CUE	Number of knowledge products (publications, tools, podcasts, etc.) developed by the Scaling team	Disseminate evidence	N/A	27 knowledge products	June 2020
EEF	Metrics on Toolkit development: number of Toolkit studies coded; number of reviews for Toolkit strands completed	Disseminate evidence	No explicit coding target; 34 reviews by March 2021	2,042 studies coded; six reviews competed	March 2020
EEF	Number of project fellows and number of country/regional jurisdictions with fellows	Develop capacity	N/A	Seven fellows across four jurisdictions	March 2020
GBC-Ed	Metrics on breadth of global education landscape analyses (e.g., number of studies, major actors, regulatory frameworks, guiding principles, strategic initiatives assessed and analyzed) or the number of stakeholders consulted	N/A	Interviews with 15–20 business leaders and 15 noncorporate entities; no other explicit targets	Interviewed 21 business leaders and 26 noncorporate entity leaders	June 2020
TFA	Metrics on volume of Community Impact Lab learning experiences: number of learning experiences; number of participants in learning experiences	Disseminate evidence; develop capacity	Three of each type of experience annually by 2020–2021: learning loops, virtual communities of practice, learning teams, expert practitioner roundtables, and virtual workshops	Experimentation with global learning experiences ongoing (with modifications because of COVID-19); numbers and types of experiences vary from initial vision	June 2020

Table A.1—Continued

Partner	Indicator	Also Indicator for Activities	Target	Status	Last Updated
TFA	Number of resources related to community impact housed in online resource bank (e.g., digital papers, case studies, snapshots, and artifacts)	Disseminate evidence	At least 50 resources curated and published annually beginning in 2019–2020	On track to meet goal for 2019–2020, despite deprioritizing this strand of work because of COVID-19	June 2020
TFA	Number of resources and tools highlighting individual partner practices in alumni leadership development curated and posted on Partner Learning Portal	Disseminate evidence	Three collective leadership resource bundles, five self-guided learning materials, and two new exemplars in each of the five core areas of leadership development added annually beginning in 2019–2020	Work ongoing (with modifications because of COVID-19); numbers and types of resources vary from initial vision	June 2020
UNW	Number of learners accessing high-quality second chance education content	Test investments	67,000 women participating in the Second Chance Education Programme via face-to-face or online learning	24,937 women	June 2020
UNW	Number of training modules/curricula developed informed by second chance education country needs assessments	Test investments	21 modules	122 modules	June 2020

NOTE: N/A in "Also Indicator for Activities" column = not an indicator for other activities; N/A in "Target" column = no explicit target; N/A in "Status" column = no reported progress to date.

Table A.2
Key Activity Indicators: Disseminate Evidence-Based Strategies

Partner	Indicator	Also Indicator for Activities	Target	Status	Last Updated
CUE	Number of knowledge products (publications, tools, podcasts, etc.) developed by the Innovations team	Curate evidence	N/A	37 knowledge products	June 2020
CUE	Number of knowledge products (publications, tools, podcasts, etc.) developed by the Analyze Data team	Curate evidence	N/A	16 knowledge products	June 2020
CUE	Number of knowledge products (publications, tools, podcasts, etc.) developed by the Scaling team	Curate evidence	N/A	27 knowledge products	June 2020
CUE	Number of CUE-initiated consultations and events related to the work of the Innovations team	Develop capacity; advocacy	N/A	275 consultations and 19 events	June 2020
CUE	Number of CUE-initiated consultations and events related to the work of the Analyze Data team	Develop capacity; advocacy	N/A	84 consultations and six events	June 2020
CUE	Number of CUE-initiated consultations and events related to the work of the Scaling team	Develop capacity; advocacy	N/A	154 consultations and 24 events	June 2020
EEF	Metrics on Toolkit development: number of Toolkit studies coded; number of reviews for Toolkit strands completed	Curate evidence	No explicit coding target; 34 reviews by March 2021	2,042 studies coded; six reviews competed	March 2020
EEF	Number of evidence hubs established	Develop capacity	One in each partner jurisdiction	None fully established; one jurisdiction with progress toward establishment	March 2020
GBC-Ed	Metrics on tool development: number of prototypes, number finalized	Develop capacity	Three to five prototypes, at least one finalized tool	N/A	June 2020

Table A.2—Continued

Partner	Indicator	Also Indicator for Activities	Target	Status	Last Updated
TFA	Metrics on volume of Community Impact Lab learning experiences: number of learning experiences; number of participants in learning experiences	Curate evidence; develop capacity	Three of each type of experience annually by 2020–2021: learning loops, virtual communities of practice, learning teams, expert practitioner roundtables, and virtual workshops	Experimentation with global learning experiences ongoing (with modifications because of COVID-19); numbers and types of experiences vary from initial vision	June 2020
TFA	Number of resources related to community impact housed in online resource bank (e.g., digital papers, case studies, snapshots, and artifacts)	Curate evidence	At least 50 resources curated and published annually beginning in 2019–2020	On track to meet goal for 2019–2020 despite deprioritizing this strand of work because of COVID-19	June 2020
TFA	Number of resources and tools highlighting individual partner practices in alumni leadership development curated and posted on Partner Learning Portal	Curate evidence	Three collective leadership resource bundles, five self-guided learning materials, and two new partner exemplars in each of the five core areas of leadership development added annually beginning in 2019–2020	Work ongoing with modifications because of COVID-19; numbers and types of resources vary from initial vision	June 2020
TFA	Metrics on activities designed to advance TFA partner learning: number of partner support initiatives undertaken by TFA specialists; number of network conferences and group learning experiences offered	Develop capacity	Four virtual learning communities for ten or more partner staff, ten in-person support initiatives to strengthen partner staff capacity, and 20 remote support initiatives annually beginning in 2019–2020	More than 15 partners engaged in person (pre–COVID-19) and more than 40 engaged virtually in 2019–2020	June 2020
UNW	Number of policy dialogues on the importance of women's right to education and vocational learning undertaken with UNW support, country and global level	Advocacy	26 country-level dialogues; two global dialogues	54 country-level dialogues; zero global dialogues	June 2020

NOTE: N/A in "Also Indicator for Activities" column = not an indicator for other activities; N/A in "Target" column = no explicit target; N/A in "Status" column = no reported progress to date.

Table A.3
Key Activity Indicators: Develop Capacity to Leverage Evidence

Partner	Indicator	Also Indicator for Activities	Target	Status	Last Updated
CUE	Number of CUE-initiated consultations and events related to the work of the Innovations team	Disseminate evidence; advocacy	N/A	275 consultations and 19 events	June 2020
CUE	Number of CUE-initiated consultations and events related to the work of the Analyze Data team	Disseminate evidence; advocacy	N/A	84 consultations and six events	June 2020
CUE	Number of CUE-initiated consultations and events related to the work of the Scaling team	Disseminate evidence; advocacy	N/A	154 consultations and 24 events	June 2020
EEF	Number of project fellows and number of country/regional jurisdictions with fellows	Curate evidence	N/A	Seven fellows across four jurisdictions	March 2020
EEF	Number of evidence hubs established	Disseminate evidence	One in each partner jurisdiction	None fully established; one jurisdiction with progress toward establishment	March 2020
GBC-Ed	Metrics on tool development: number of prototypes, number finalized	Disseminate evidence	Three to five prototypes; at least one finalized tool	N/A	June 2020
TFA	Metrics on volume of Community Impact Lab learning experiences: number of learning experiences, number of participants in learning experiences	Curate evidence; disseminate evidence	Three of each type of experience annually by 2020–2021: learning loops, virtual communities of practice, learning teams, expert practitioner roundtables, and virtual workshops	Experimentation with global learning experiences ongoing (with modifications because of COVID-19); numbers and types of experiences vary from initial vision	June 2020

Table A.3—Continued

Partner	Indicator	Also Indicator for Activities	Target	Status	Last Updated
TFA	Metrics on activities designed to advance TFA partner learning: number of partner support initiatives undertaken by TFA specialists; number of network conferences and group learning experiences offered	Disseminate evidence	Four virtual learning communities for ten or more partner staff, ten in-person support initiatives to strengthen partner staff capacity, and 20 remote support initiatives annually beginning in 2019–2020	More than 15 partners engaged in person (pre–COVID-19) and more than 40 engaged virtually in 2019–2020	June 2020
TFA	Number of communities participating in community-level progress matrix and that have established local indicators for progress	N/A	50 communities experimenting with approaches to measure community-level progress by 2020–2021, with indicators for measuring progress identified in a similar number of communities by 2021–2022	At least 20 communities experimenting with measures of community-level progress, including six communities engaged in in-depth reflection	June 2020
UNW	Number of physical spaces or Women's Empowerment Hubs/ community spaces providing access to second chance education e-learning platform and other second chance education learning opportunities established with UNW support	Test investments	45 physical spaces	41 physical spaces	June 2020

NOTE: N/A in "Also Indicator for Activities" column = not an indicator for other activities; N/A in "Target" column = no explicit target; N/A in "Status" column = no reported progress to date.

Table A.4
Key Activity Indicators: Advocate to Develop Enabling Environments

Partner	Indicator	Also Indicator for Activities	Target	Status	Last Updated
CUE	Number of CUE-initiated consultations and events related to the work of the Innovations team	Disseminate evidence; develop capacity	N/A	275 consultations and 19 events	June 2020
CUE	Number of CUE-initiated consultations and events related to the work of the Analyze Data team	Disseminate evidence; develop capacity	N/A	84 consultations and six events	June 2020
CUE	Number of CUE-initiated consultations and events related to the work of the Scaling team	Disseminate evidence; develop capacity	N/A	154 consultations and 24 events	June 2020
EEF	Number of engagements with policymakers	N/A	N/A	12 policymaker engagements explicitly documented	March 2020
UNW	Number of policy dialogues on the importance of women's right to education and vocational learning undertaken with UNW support, country and global level	Disseminate evidence	26 country-level dialogues; two global dialogues	54 country-level dialogues; zero global dialogues	June 2020
UNW	Number of awareness and advocacy campaigns on the importance of young women's right to education and vocational learning undertaken with UNW support, country and global level	N/A	13 country-level campaigns, three global campaigns	16 country-level campaigns; zero global campaigns	June 2020

NOTE: N/A in "Also Indicator for Activities" column = not an indicator for other activities; N/A in "Target" column = no explicit target; N/A in "Status" column = no reported progress to date; TBD in "Status" column = progress reported but not yet quantified.

Table A.5
Key Activity Indicators: Test Potentially Transformative Investments

Partner	Indicator	Also Indicator for Activities	Target	Status	Last Updated
EEF	Metrics on volume of trials: number of applications to conduct trials; number of trials conducted	N/A	Two trials in each partner jurisdiction	Ten applications across three jurisdictions; three funded trials in one jurisdiction	March 2020
UNW	Number of learners accessing high-quality second chance education content	Curate evidence	67,000 women participating in the Second Chance Education Programme via face-to-face or online learning	24,937 women	June 2020
UNW	Number of training modules/curricula developed informed by second chance education country needs assessments	Curate evidence	21 modules	122 modules	June 2020
UNW	Number of physical spaces or Women's Empowerment Hubs/community spaces providing access to second chance education e-learning platform and other second chance education learning opportunities established with UNW support	Develop capacity	45 physical spaces	41 physical spaces	June 2020

NOTE: N/A in "Also Indicator for Activities" column = not an indicator for other activities; N/A in "Target" column = no explicit target; N/A in "Status" column = no reported progress to date.

Table A.6
Key Interim Outcome Indicators: Increased Availability of Data and Evidence

Partner	Indicator	Also Indicator for Interim Outcomes	Activities Leading to Interim Outcome	Target	Status	Last Updated
CUE	Number of externally initiated engagements related to the work of the Innovations team, such as requests (participated in and declined) from the media, briefings, panels, etc.	Empowered leaders and actors	Curate evidence; disseminate evidence; develop capacity; advocacy	N/A	93 engagements	June 2020
CUE	Number of externally initiated engagements related to the work of the Analyze Data team, such as requests (participated in and declined) from the media, briefings, panels, etc.	Empowered leaders and actors	Curate evidence; disseminate evidence; develop capacity; advocacy	N/A	78 engagements	June 2020
CUE	Number of externally initiated engagements related to the work of the Scaling team, such as requests (participated in and declined) from the media, briefings, panels, etc.	Empowered leaders and actors	Curate evidence; disseminate evidence; develop capacity; advocacy	N/A	34 engagements	June 2020
EEF	Rate of use of Toolkit to make resource allocation or school improvement decisions, as measured by proportion of school-based and system leadership staff reporting decisionmaking based on Toolkit evidence	Informed decisionmaking	Curate evidence; disseminate evidence	N/A	N/A	March 2020
EEF	Number of publications of trial results	N/A	Test investments	N/A	N/A	March 2020
TFA	Reach of stories and reports prepared for dissemination in public channels as measured by number of media mentions and number of attendees at public events	N/A	Curate evidence; disseminate evidence	N/A	N/A	June 2020
UNW	Number and percentage increase in employed/entrepreneur women among program graduates	Empowered leaders and actors	Curate evidence; develop capacity; test investments	17,500 women	5,763 women	June 2020

NOTE: N/A in "Also Indicator for Activities" column = not an indicator for other activities; N/A in "Target" column = no explicit target; N/A in "Status" column = no reported progress to date; TBD in "Status" column = progress reported but not yet quantified.

Table A.7
Key Interim Outcome Indicators: More-Informed Decisionmaking

Partner	Indicator	Also Indicator for Interim Outcomes	Activities Leading to Interim Outcome	Target	Status	Last Updated
EEF	Rate of use of Toolkit to make resource allocation or school improvement decisions, as measured by proportion of school-based and system leadership staff reporting decisionmaking based on Toolkit evidence	Availability of data and evidence	Curate evidence; disseminate evidence	N/A	N/A	March 2020
EEF	Metrics on the translation of engagement with policymakers into policy	Empowered leaders and actors	Advocacy	N/A	N/A	March 2020
GBC-Ed	Metrics on use of such tools as the number of business users; number of workshops and training sessions for environmental, social, and governance professionals; and the number of professionals trained	Empowered leaders and actors	Curate evidence; disseminate evidence; develop capacity	Ten to 15 companies and ten noncorporate entities using tools developed	N/A	June 2020
GBC-Ed	Metrics related to dissemination and implementation of guidance material for noncorporate stakeholders in education	Empowered leaders and actors	Disseminate evidence; advocacy	Surveys/interviews of private-sector engagement team/ staff of three major global education funds, ten UN agencies and international organizations, and ten donor and developing country partners	N/A	June 2020

Table A.7—Continued

Partner	Indicator	Also Indicator for Interim Outcomes	Activities Leading to Interim Outcome	Target	Status	Last Updated
TFA	Network partner staff and global stakeholders report that their knowledge increased after engagements with the Community Impact Lab as measured by responses to surveys	Empowered leaders and actors	Curate evidence; disseminate evidence; develop capacity	N/A, seeking improvement over time	87 percent of 170 lab learning experience participants reported that their understanding increased as a result of the experience	June 2020
UNW	Number of new, revised, or in active review/discussion legislative frameworks, policies, or revised budgetary allocations that promote second chance education and vocational training opportunities for women developed and/or being implemented in second chance education countries	Empowered leaders and actors	Disseminate evidence; advocacy	Nine frameworks or policies (general); six revised budgetary allocations	Nine frameworks or policies (general); zero revised budgetary allocations	June 2020

NOTE: N/A in "Also Indicator for Activities" column = not an indicator for other activities; N/A in "Target" column = no explicit target; N/A in "Status" column = no reported progress to date.

Table A.8
Key Interim Outcome Indicators: Networks of Purposeful Collaboration

Partner	Indicator	Also Indicator for Interim Outcomes	Activities Leading to Interim Outcome	Target	Status	Last Updated
EEF	Number of annual engagements between evidence hubs and supported schools (both formal meetings and otherwise)	Empowered leaders and actors	Disseminate evidence; develop capacity	50 formal engagements per evidence hub annually	N/A	March 2020
EEF	Number of organizations supported to take on the role of evidence brokers	N/A	Develop capacity	N/A	Six formal partners; more than 40 organizations attended most recent global partnership workshop	March 2020
TFA	Reach of TFA alumni network as measured by total number of alumni, percentage working in education, and percentage working in roles that expand opportunities for children in high-need communities	Empowered leaders and actors	Develop capacity	N/A, seeking improvement over time	75,100 alumni; 72 percent working in education; 66 percent working to expand opportunity in underserved communities	June 2020
TFA	Engagement of TFA alumni network as measured by number and percentage of alumni responding to survey, percentage increase in effective alumni leadership, and percentage increase in Net Promoter Score	Empowered leaders and actors	Disseminate evidence; develop capacity	N/A, seeking improvement over time	19 partners opting in and a median response rate of 45 percent; over 82 percent of alumni strongly agreed or agreed to the majority of the mindset questions	June 2020
UNW	Number of partnerships established identifying community spaces/ empowerment hubs with local governments, communities, and private-sector partners to create safe learning spaces	N/A	Develop capacity; test investments	70 partnerships	77 partnerships	June 2020
UNW	Number of peer networks for women established, with UNW support, country and global level	N/A	Develop capacity; test investments	21 country-level networks; one global network	20 country-level networks; zero global network	June 2020

NOTE: N/A in "Also Indicator for Activities" column = not an indicator for other activities; N/A in "Target" column = no explicit target; N/A in "Status" column = no reported progress to date.

Table A.9
Key Interim Outcome Indicators: Empowered Thought Leaders and Local Actors

Partner	Indicator	Also Indicator for Interim Outcomes	Activities Leading to Interim Outcome	Target	Status	Last Updated
CUE	Number of externally initiated engagements related to the work of the Innovations team, such as requests (participated in and declined) from the media, briefings, panels, etc.	Availability of data and evidence	Curate evidence; disseminate evidence; develop capacity; advocacy	N/A	93 engagements	June 2020
CUE	Number of externally initiated engagements related to the work of the Analyze Data team, such as requests (participated in and declined) from the media, briefings, panels, etc.	Availability of data and evidence	Curate evidence; disseminate evidence; develop capacity; advocacy	N/A	78 engagements	June 2020
CUE	Number of externally initiated engagements related to the work of the Scaling team, such as requests (participated in and declined) from the media, briefings, panels, etc.	Availability of data and evidence	Curate evidence; disseminate evidence; develop capacity; advocacy	N/A	34 engagements	June 2020
EEF	Number of annual engagements between evidence hubs and supported schools (both formal meetings and otherwise)	Networks established	Disseminate evidence; develop capacity	50 formal engagements per evidence hub annually	N/A	March 2020
EEF	Metrics on the translation of engagement with policymakers into policy	Informed decisionmaking	Advocacy	N/A	N/A	March 2020

Table A.9—Continued

Partner	Indicator	Also Indicator for Interim Outcomes	Activities Leading to Interim Outcome	Target	Status	Last Updated
GBC-Ed	Metrics on use of tools such as the number of business users, number of workshops and training sessions for environmental, social, and governance professionals, or the number of professionals trained	Informed decisionmaking	Curate evidence; disseminate evidence; develop capacity	Ten to 15 companies and ten noncorporate entities using tools developed	N/A	June 2020
GBC-Ed	Metrics related to dissemination and implementation of guidance material for noncorporate stakeholders in education	Informed decisionmaking	Disseminate evidence; advocacy	Surveys/interviews of private-sector engagement team/staff of three major global education funds, ten UN agencies and international organizations, and ten donor and developing country partners	N/A	June 2020
TFA	Network partner staff and global stakeholders report that their knowledge increased after engagements with the Community Impact Lab as measured by responses to surveys	Informed decisionmaking	Curate evidence; disseminate evidence; develop capacity	N/A, seeking improvement over time	87 percent of 170 lab learning experience participants reported that their understanding increased as a result of the experience	June 2020
TFA	Reach of TFA alumni network as measured by total number of alumni, percentage working in education, and percentage working in roles that expand opportunities for children in high need communities	Networks established	Develop capacity	N/A, seeking improvement over time	75,100 alumni; 72 percent working in education, 66 percent working to expand opportunity in under-served communities	June 2020

Table A.9—Continued

Partner	Indicator	Also Indicator for Interim Outcomes	Activities Leading to Interim Outcome	Target	Status	Last Updated
TFA	Engagement of TFA alumni network as measured by number and percentage of alumni responding to survey; percentage increase in effective alumni leadership, and percentage increase in Net Promoter Score	Networks established	Disseminate evidence; develop capacity	N/A, seeking improvement over time	19 partners opting in and a median response rate of 45 percent; over 82 percent of alumni strongly agreed or agreed to the majority of the mindset questions	June 2020
UNW	Number and percentage increase in employed/ entrepreneur women among program graduates	Availability of data and evidence	Curate evidence; develop capacity; test investments	17,500 women	5,763 women	June 2020
UNW	Number of new, revised, or in active review/discussion legislative frameworks, policies, or revised budgetary allocations that promote second chance education and vocational training opportunities for women developed and/or being implemented in second chance education countries	Informed decisionmaking	Disseminate evidence; advocacy	Nine frameworks or policies (general); six revised budgetary allocations	Nine frameworks or policies (general); zero revised budgetary allocations	June 2020

NOTE: N/A in "Also Indicator for Activities" column = not an indicator for other activities; N/A in "Target" column = no explicit target; N/A in "Status" column = no reported progress to date.

Table A.10
Long-Term Outcome Indicator Dashboard

Indicator	Long-Term Outcome for Which Indicator	Average for Ten Key BHP Foundation Countries	Last Updated
Literacy rate, youth (percentage of people ages 15–24), by sex	Improved educational attainment	96.7 percent male; 96.1 percent female	2015–2019
Persistence to last grade of primary school, by sex	Improved educational attainment	91.4 percent male; 92.2 percent female	2016–2018
Adolescents out of school (percentage of lower secondary school age), by sex	Improved educational attainment	11.6 percent male; 11.1 percent female	2013–2019
Government expenditure on education (percentage of gross domestic product)	More and more-efficient educational investments	4.2 percent	2013–2019
Government expenditure on education (percentage of government expenditure)	More and more-efficient educational investments	15.0 percent	2013–2019

NOTES: The countries include in the "Average for Ten Key BHP Foundation Countries" average are Australia, Cameroon, Chile, India, Jordan, Mexico, Peru, the Philippines, Spain, and the United Kingdom. The last updated date varies by country; the averages are calculated for the countries for which data are available.

APPENDIX B

Interviews and Network Analyses Research Approach

Partner Interviews

To elicit details about partner organizations' project activities and progress, we conducted an initial set of phone and video interviews in spring 2020 with project leaders of each of the five partner organizations. We sent a brief outline of the main topics to be addressed, and each organization determined the project leaders who would participate. In total, we interviewed 14 individuals across the five organizations (with one to four participants per interview). The interview protocol focused on learning about the partners' key strategies for achieving their project goals. This entailed probing into key activities that propel the BHP Foundation's theory of change (e.g., curating and disseminating evidence, engaging in local capacity building, developing enabling environments, testing transformative innovations). We also sought clarification on the key indicators the partners will use to assess progress toward their intended outcomes. In fall 2020, we conducted a second round of interviews with the funded partners. This time, we spoke with 12 individuals across the five organizations. This interview protocol addressed progress the partners have made in each stream of their work since spring. We also focused on challenges project teams have encountered and their mitigation strategies, as well as lessons learned that may inform subsequent activities or be applicable across partners.

To gain a big-picture understanding of the Program, we conducted individual interviews with three members of the BHP Foundation leadership in June 2020. The interview protocol was composed of three major sections. The first section was focused on mapping the Program's theory of change. We sought to better understand how the BHP Foundation envisions it will change education worldwide, particularly for target populations. We asked about the impetus and rationale for the Program; the Program's intended impacts (within and outside its sphere of influence), beneficiaries, and outcomes; indicators that BHP Foundation staff believe will gauge how they and their partners are advancing toward these outcomes; and resources and conditions needed to support Program activities. The second section focused on the five funded partners—how the BHP Foundation selected the partners and projects, how they fit into the BHP Foundation's overall strategy and vision for the Program, and what activities and interim outcomes are expected of the partners. In the third section, we aimed to compare the BHP Foundation's Program with similar investments and programs.

Before each interview, we reviewed available documents, including the BHP Foundation's original invitation to tender, each partner's original proposal in response to the invitation, the Year 1 and available Year 2 (2020) quarterly reports that partners submitted to the BHP Foundation, and other artifacts of the project work (e.g., needs assessments conducted, spreadsheet of outcome indicators, disseminated products). We distilled information from these sources into brief summaries to facilitate understanding of each project and make comparisons among projects. Moreover, we used this information to develop and customize the interview protocol for each partner to help frame the conversation and move our questions beyond surface-level fact-finding. For example, upon identifying the ways in which CUE was engaging in capacity building, we asked why this was a key strategy, what activities supported this strategy, to what extent these activities have been successful, and what these successes are attributed to. We were able to follow up on challenges noted in reports and request richer details. In preparation for the interviews, we met to check understanding of each partner's project goals and strategies and identify particularly useful probes. After each interview, we debriefed as a team; we converged on key learnings and emergent themes and noted any items requiring clarification.

With interviewees' consent, we recorded each interview and took detailed notes to facilitate analysis. After each round of interviews, we imported the detailed notes into Dedoose 8.3.17, a cross-platform internet application for analysis of qualitative data. Coding followed established qualitative research procedures (Denzin and Lincoln, 2003; Lincoln and Guba, 1985; Miles, Huberman, and Saldaña, 2019; Strauss and Corbin, 1994). We developed an initial top-level coding scheme that was guided by our interview protocol and theory-of-change constructs and that reflected emergent themes gleaned from a review of the partners' reports. The qualitative lead coded and analyzed the interview data.

Analysis involved a systematic review of excerpts coded to each key node (e.g., corresponding to the five key activities and strategies identified in the theory of change), along with codes for capturing challenges, facilitators, and lessons learned. We drew on established techniques (Bernard, Wutich, and Ryan, 2016; Ryan and Bernard, 2003), including looking for repetitions, similarities, and differences between interviews, to identify themes. To ensure the credibility of our findings, we triangulated across interviews and sought confirmatory and disconfirming evidence in documents (Denzin, 2006).

To ensure the accuracy of our findings, we elicited the input of the BHP Foundation and its funded partners at multiple points in the evaluation. For example, in addition to formal data collection activities (i.e., interviews), we engaged partners in email exchanges in which we sought their confirmation or suggested revisions to our draft indicator framework or we requested updated data, particularly for the tables in

Appendix A. We also provided a completed draft of the report to the BHP Foundation and its partners for fact-checking. Their responsiveness has helped improve the accuracy of the report.

Network Analysis

To collect data for our analysis of UNW's networks of partner organizations involved in second chance education in Mexico, we developed questionnaires for leaders at UNW and their three key implementing partners (one in each region of Mexico). At each organization, we worked primarily with a single point of contact, who conferred with colleagues in their own organization and then summarized for us their view of the collaborations between organizations involved in the second chance education work.

UNW and its key implementing partners first prepared a list of all the organizations that it viewed as contributors to the second chance education work. Then representatives from UNW provided our primary data about perceived interactions between all of the organizations. For each of the four goals of the second chance education work, UNW completed a matrix (in a spreadsheet document) in which it indicated whether it perceived interactions (yes or no) between each potential pairing of the listed organizations.

UNW reported some degree of interaction between itself and every organization included in our network analysis, and additionally reported the importance of its own partnerships (on a one-to-five scale) with each organization with respect to each of its goals. However, in our final visualizations, we show UNW's ties only to organizations that UNW reported as the most important partnerships to each goal; this was to avoid cluttered diagrams (because our focus was on how other organizations work together to enhance UNW efforts).

To partially validate the views of UNW representatives, we also asked representatives from each of UNW's three key implementing partners in Mexico to fill out a more focused spreadsheet; this spreadsheet noted whether the organization interacted with each of the other listed organizations in connection to each of the four second chance education goals. In our visualizations, we report on ties between key partners and other organizations only in cases where they themselves reported a connection. Although UNW and the key partners usually identified the same connections between organizations, there were some discrepancies. In most cases, this was caused by differing views of what constituted a connection or collaboration relevant to the second chance education work, rather than to lack of awareness of a connection between organizations. This cross-validation of the data with the key implementing partners provided a check on many, but by no means all, of the connections between organizations that UNW reported. Therefore, our network visualizations are still heavily dependent on the perceptions of UNW representatives and are potentially an incomplete picture of the ecosystem of organizations and how they interacted to facilitate the second chance education work.

We also collected a variety of characteristics of each organization, including the various types of work that they do (e.g., provide learning content, provide employment opportunities, provide hardware or software) toward the second chance education goals; the organizations' status as governmental or nongovernmental agencies or organizations; and the region in which they operate. In collaboration with UNW, we iterated various permutations of network visualizations, examining the distributions of organizations with different characteristics and which were most relevant to the structure of connected organizations. Our final network visualizations do not detail all of these characteristics but instead focus on those characteristics that were most related to the connections between organizations (most notably the regions in which they operated).

APPENDIX C

Comparator Organization Analysis Approach

To identify comparator case studies, we first developed a longlist of potential comparators based on desk research. This aim of this desk research was to identify a variety of different potential comparator organizations that shared the BHP Foundation's evidence-to-practice goals, even if these organizations were not necessarily funders or focused on the education sector. This included other private foundations active within the education sector; it also included broader nongovernmental organizations working within this space, as well as organizations operating outside education that shared the BHP Foundation program's evidence-to-practice goals. The longlist of potential comparators captured information on the nature of each organization's work, its sectoral and geographical focus, its relevance to key BHP Foundation program goals, and the strength of the documentation available.

Drawing on this information, we narrowed the longlist down to a shortlist of six comparator case studies. We chose our case studies because of their relevance to the BHP Foundation's program; we included both direct comparators and more-indirect comparators because we wanted to include a diverse set of cross-organizational and cross-sectoral comparisons. Our final selection spanned various types of organizations, including corporate foundations working within the education investment landscape, education-focused nongovernmental organizations, foundations focusing on evidence-to-practice initiatives in other fields (such as health), and wider social investment initiatives or research programs that share the BHP Foundation's evidence-to-practice goals.

Once the six comparator cases had been selected, we developed a common analytical template. The template helped to structure our research into the individual cases and to facilitate later cross-analysis. The template identified the following key areas of interest that would be explored for each comparator:

1. key features of the comparator, including strategic objectives and theory of change
2. key BHP Foundation program–relevant interventions
3. evaluation approaches
4. key achievements
5. lessons learned.

Research for the comparator case studies relied on two methods: desk research and interviews. Desk research included key documents produced by the comparator organization, such as strategy documents, logic models and theories of change, reports (including annual reports), evaluation frameworks and evaluations, and broader website material and gray literature. Interviews were focused on individuals with direct involvement in the comparator organization's strategic planning, program implementation, or evaluation. Our interviews had a semistructured approach, with questions following a protocol based around the common analytical template but tailored to the specifics of each comparator. Interviews were conducted for all six comparators. In total, we interviewed 13 individuals across the six comparator organizations.

Having developed a detailed understanding of each comparator using the common template, including individual case study write-ups, we conducted internal workshops. Researchers took an iterative and emergent approach to group together emerging findings and recognize cross-cutting themes and commonalities. Cross-cutting themes identified shared challenges and opportunities faced by organizations working in a variety of fields and scales; themes were grouped under two overarching categories: *strategy and implementation* and *evaluation approaches*. Further analysis of the cross-cutting themes led to the identification of different models and approaches used by comparators for each theme. The resulting themes and typologies formed the basis of the cross-analytical write-up included in this report.

Bibliography

Abdul Latif Jameel Poverty Action Lab, "About Us," webpage, undated-a. As of March 11, 2021:
https://www.povertyactionlab.org/about-j-pal

———, "Evidence to Policy," webpage, undated-b. As of March 11, 2021:
https://www.povertyactionlab.org/evidence-to-policy

Alliance—*See* Alliance for Useful Evidence.

Alliance for Useful Evidence, "About Us," webpage, undated. As of March 11, 2021:
https://www.alliance4usefulevidence.org/about-us/aboutus

———, "Theory of Change," flow chart, July 2018. As of March 11, 2021:
https://www.alliance4usefulevidence.org/publication/alliance-for-useful-evidence-theory-of-change

Annenberg Foundation, "The Annenberg Challenge," webpage, undated. As of March 7, 2021:
https://annenberg.org/initiatives/the-annenberg-challenge

Asian Development Bank, "ADB's Work in the Education Sector," webpage, undated. As of March 7, 2021:
https://www.adb.org/sectors/education/adb-support-education

Bamberger, Michael, and Eleanor Hewitt, *Monitoring and Evaluating Urban Development Programs: A Handbook for Program Managers and Researchers*, Washington, D.C.: World Bank, 1986.

Bamberger, Michael, Vijayendra Rao, and Michael Woodcock, "Using Mixed Methods in Monitoring and Evaluation: Experiences from International Development," World Bank, Policy Research Working Paper 5245, 2010.

Barrett, Christopher B, and Michael R. Carter, "The Power and Pitfalls of Experiments in Development Economics: Some Non-Random Reflections," *Applied Economic Perspectives and Policy*, Vol. 32, No. 4, 2010, pp. 515–548.

Battilana, Julie, and Tiziana Casciaro, "The Network Secrets of Great Change Agents," *Harvard Business Review,* July–August 2013, pp. 62–68. As of March 7, 2021:
https://hbr.org/2013/07/the-network-secrets-of-great-change-agents

Bernard, H. Russell, Amber Wutich, and Gery W. Ryan, *Analyzing Qualitative Data: Systematic Approaches,* Thousand Oaks, Calif.: SAGE Publications, 2016.

Bill & Melinda Gates Foundation, *Global Education Learning Initiative: Theory of Action*, Seattle, Wash., undated-a, Not available to the general public.

———, "How We Work: Evaluation Policy," webpage, undated-b. As of April 2, 2021:
https://www.gatesfoundation.org/How-We-Work/General-Information/Evaluation-Policy

———, "Global Education Program Strategy Overview," webpage, undated-c. As of March 18, 2021:
https://www.gatesfoundation.org/our-work/programs/global-growth-and-opportunity/global-education-program

———, "Global Libraries," webpage, undated-d. As of March 7, 2021:
https://www.gatesfoundation.org/our-work/programs/global-development/global-libraries

Borgatti, Stephen P., Martin G. Everett, and Jeffrey J. Johnson, *Analyzing Social Networks,* Thousand Oaks, Calif.: SAGE Publications, 2018.

Center for Universal Education, Brookings Institution, *Annual Report for the BHP Foundation Covering Grant Period 7/1/19 Through 6/30/20*, Washington, D.C., 2020, Not available to the general public.

Cross, Rob, and Robert Thomas, "Managing Yourself: A Smarter Way to Network," *Harvard Business Review*, July–August 2011, pp. 149–153.

Csermely, Peter, András London, Ling-Yun Wu, and Brian Uzzi, "Structure and Dynamics of Core/Periphery Networks," *Journal of Complex Networks*, Vol. 1, No. 2, 2013, pp. 93–123.

CUE—*See* Center for Universal Education, Brookings Institution.

Culbertson, Shelly, Gabriella C. Gonzalez, and Nupur Nanda, *The Appalachia Partnership Initiative's Investments in Education, Workforce Development, and the Community: Technical Appendixes*, Santa Monica, Calif.: RAND Corporation, RR-2017/1-CHC, 2017. As of November 18, 2020:
https://www.rand.org/pubs/research_reports/RR2017z1.html

Cyr, Helene, *Akazi Kanoze 2: Cost Analysis Report*, Waltham, Mass.: Education Development Center, 2017. As of March 11, 2021:
http://idd.edc.org/resources/publications/akazi-kanoze-2-cost-analysis-report

Denzin, Norman K., *Sociological Methods: A Sourcebook*, New York: Routledge, 2006.

Denzin, Norman K., and Yvonna S. Lincoln, *Collecting and Interpreting Qualitative Materials*, Thousand Oaks, Calif.: SAGE Publications, 2003.

Doran, George T., "There's a S.M.A.R.T. Way to Write Management's Goals and Objectives," *Management Review*, Vol. 70, 1981, pp. 35–36.

EDC—*See* Education Development Center.

EDCTP—*See* European and Developing Counties Clinical Trials Partnership.

Education Commission, Center for Global Education at Asia Society, Results for Development, Teach for All, Boston Consulting Group, and World Innovation Summit for Education, *Investing in Knowledge Sharing to Advance SDG 4*, New York: Education Commission, 2018. As of February 4, 2021:
https://educationcommission.org/wp-content/uploads/2018/09/Investing-in-Knowledge-Sharing-to-Advance-SDG-4.pdf

Education Commission, International Commission on Financing Global Education Opportunity, *The Learning Generation: Investing in Education for a Changing World*, New York, 2016. As of February 4, 2021:
https://report.educationcommission.org/wp-content/uploads/2016/09/Learning_Generation_Full_Report.pdf

Education Development Center, "About EDC," webpage, undated-a. As of March 11, 2021:
https://www.edc.org/about

———, "Read Right Now (RRN)," webpage, undated-b. As of March 11, 2021:
https://www.edc.org/read-right-now

———, "Work Ready Now (WRN)," webpage, undated-c. As of March 11, 2021:
https://www.edc.org/work-ready-now

———, *Akazi Kanoze Youth Livelihoods Project, Final Report 2009–2016*, Waltham, Mass., 2016. As of March 11, 2021:
https://www.edc.org/akazi-kanoze-youth-livelihoods-project-final-report

Education Endowment Foundation, *Building a Global Evidence Eco-System for Teaching: Year 2 Project Report*, London, 2020, Not available to the general public.

Edwards, Sophie, "Is the Global Education Sector Heading Toward Fragmentation," Devex, August 23, 2018. As of March 11, 2021:
https://www.devex.com/news/is-the-global-education-sector-heading-toward-fragmentation-93270

EEF—*See* Education Endowment Foundation.

European and Developing Counties Clinical Trials Partnership, *EDCTP Strategic Business Plan for 2014–2024*, The Hague: Netherlands, May 2018. As of March 18, 2021:
https://www.edctp.org/web/app/uploads/2018/06/
EDCTP-Strategic-Business-Plan-2014-2024-May-2018.pdf

———, *Measuring Results of EDCTP: A Guiding Document for Monitoring and Evaluation of EDCTP2 Programme*, The Hague: Netherlands, 2019, Not available to the general public.

Fulk, Janet, and Brian K. Boyd, "Emerging Theories of Communication in Organizations," *Journal of Management*, Vol. 17, No. 2, 1991, pp. 407–446.

Gates Foundation—*See* Bill & Melinda Gates Foundation.

Green, Harold D., Jr., and Stanley Wasserman, "Network Analysis: A Definitional Guide to Important Concepts," in Todd D. Little, ed., *The Oxford Handbook of Quantitative Methods in Psychology*, Vol. 1, Oxford: Oxford University Press, 2013.

Haims, Marla C., Melinda Moore, Harold D. Green, Jr., and Cynthia C. Clapp-Wincek, *Developing a Prototype Handbook for Monitoring and Evaluating Department of Defense Humanitarian Assistance Projects*, Santa Monica, Calif.: RAND Corporation, TR-784-OSD, 2011. As November 18, 2020:
https://www.rand.org/pubs/technical_reports/TR784.html

Hanushek, Eric A., and Dennis D. Kimko, "Schooling, Labor-Force Quality, and the Growth of Nations," *American Economic Review*, Vol. 90, No. 5, December 2000, pp. 1184–1208.

Johannisson, Bengt, "Beyond Process and Structure: Social Exchange Networks," *International Studies of Management and Organization*, Vol. 17, No. 1, 1987, pp. 3–23.

J-PAL—*See* Abdul Latif Jameel Poverty Action Lab.

Kadushin, Charles, *Understanding Social Networks: Theories, Concepts, and Findings*, New York: Oxford University Press, 2012.

Kezar, Adrianna, "Higher Education Change and Social Networks: A Review of Research," *Journal of Higher Education*, Vol. 85, No. 1, 2014, pp. 91–125.

Kitts, James, "Mobilizing in Black Boxes: Social Networks and Participation in Social Movement Organizations," *Mobilization: An International Quarterly*, Vol. 5, No. 2, 2000, pp. 241–257.

KPMG International, *Bill & Melinda Gates Foundation: Consolidated Financial Statements, December 31, 2019 and 2018 (With Independent Auditors' Report Theron)*, May 1, 2020. As of March 7, 2021:
https://docs.gatesfoundation.org/Documents/F_087119F-1B_19_BillMelindaGatesFoundation_FS.PDF

Krueger, Alan B., and Mikael Lindahl, "Education for Growth: Why and for Whom?" National Bureau of Economic Research, Working Paper 7591, March 2000. As of March 7, 2021:
https://www.nber.org/papers/w7591

LaPira, Timothy M., Herschel F. Thomas, and Frank R. Baumgartner, "The Two Worlds of Lobbying: Washington Lobbyists in the Core and on the Periphery," *Interest Groups and Advocacy*, Vol. 3, 2014, pp. 219–245.

Leonardi, Paul, and Noshir Contractor, "Better People Analytics," *Harvard Business Review*, November–December 2018, pp. 70–81. As of March 7, 2021:
https://hbr.org/2018/11/better-people-analytics

Lincoln, Yvonna Sessions, and Egon G. Guba, *Naturalistic Inquiry*, Beverly Hills, Calif.: SAGE Publications, 1985.

Mastercard Foundation, "Mission and Values," webpage, undated-a. As of March 11, 2021:
https://mastercardfdn.org/foundation/mission-vision

———, "Young Africa Works, Mastercard Foundation Strategy: 2018–2030," webpage, undated-b. As of March 11, 2021:
https://mastercardfdn.org/strategy

———, "Mastercard Foundation to Enable Three Million Youth to Access Employment Opportunities in Senegal," press release, September 24, 2019. As of March 11, 2021:
https://mastercardfdn.org/mastercard-foundation-to-enable-three-million-youth-to-access-employment-opportunities-in-senegal

Mayne, John, *Contribution Analysis: An Approach to Exploring Cause and Effect*, Institutional Learning and Change Initiative, ILAC Brief 16, May 2008.

McDavid, James C., and Laura R. L. Hawthorn, *Program Evaluation and Performance Measurement: An Introduction to Practice*, Thousand Oaks, Calif.: SAGE Publications, 2006.

Miles, Matthew B., A. Michael Huberman, and Johnny Saldaña, *Qualitative Data Analysis: A Methods Sourcebook*, 4th ed., Thousand Oaks, Calif.: SAGE Publications, 2019.

Monge, Peter R., and Noshir S. Contractor, *Theories of Communication Networks*, New York: Oxford University Press, 2003.

Mostafa, Mohamed M., "Information Diffusion in Halal Food Social Media: A Social Network Approach," *Journal of International Consumer Marketing*, 2020, pp. 1–21.

Mthiyane, Helen, *Theory of Change*, London: Alliance for Useful Evidence, June 2018. As of March 11, 2021:
https://www.alliance4usefulevidence.org/wp-content/uploads/2018/06/A4UE-Theory-of-change-narrative.pdf

Mthiyane, Helen, and Jonathan Breckon, *Our Impact, 2016–2019*, London: Alliance for Useful Evidence, January 2020. As of March 11, 2021:
https://www.alliance4usefulevidence.org/publication/our-impact-2016-2019

OECD—*See* Organisation for Economic Co-operation and Development.

Organisation for Economic Co-operation and Development, *Education at a Glance 2020: OECD Indicators*, Paris, 2020a. As of March 7, 2021:
http://www.oecd.org/education/
OECD-Work-Education-Skills-Policy-Products-Services-for-Countries.pdf

———, *PISA 2018 Results: Effective Policies, Successful Schools*, Vol. V, Paris, September 29, 2020b. As of March 7, 2021:
http://www.oecd.org/publications/pisa-2018-results-volume-v-ca768d40-en.htm

Partnership to Strengthen Innovation and Practice in Secondary Education, homepage, undated. As of March 11, 2021:
https://psipse.org/home

Pieterse, Pieternella, "Does the RCT Tail Wag the Implementation Dog?" *World Development*, Vol. 127, 2020.

Pritchett, Lant, Michael Woolcock, and Matt Andrews, "Capability Traps? The Mechanisms of Persistent Implementation Failure," Center for Global Development, Working Paper 234, December 7, 2010.

———, "Looking Like a State: Techniques of Persistent Failure in State Capability for Implementation," *Journal of Development Studies*, Vol. 49, No. 1, 2013, pp. 1–18.

PSIPSE—*See* Partnership to Strengthen Innovation and Practice in Secondary Education.

Rimal, Rajiv N., and Kevin Real, "How Behaviors Are Influenced by Perceived Norms: A Test of the Theory of Normative Social Behavior," *Communication Research*, Vol. 32, No. 3, 2005, pp. 389–414.

Robins, Garry L., *Doing Social Network Research: Network-Based Research Design for Social Scientists*, Thousand Oaks, Calif.: SAGE Publications, 2015.

Robinson, Jenny Perlman, Rebecca Winthrop, and Eileen McGivney, *Millions Learning: Scaling Up Quality Education in Developing Countries*, Washington, D.C.: Center for Universal Education at Brookings, 2016. As of March 8, 2021:
https://www.brookings.edu/wp-content/uploads/2016/04/FINAL-Millions-Learning-Report-1.pdf

Rogers, Everett M., "New Product Adoption and Diffusion," *Journal of Consumer Research*, Vol. 2, No. 4, 1976, pp. 290–301.

———, *Diffusion of Innovations*, 4th ed., New York: Simon and Schuster, 2010.

Ryan, Gery W., and H. Russell Bernard, "Techniques to Identify Themes," *Field Methods*, Vol. 15, No. 1, 2003, pp. 85–109.

Sahlberg, P., "Education Reform for Raising Economic Competitiveness," *Journal of Educational Change*, Vol. 7, No. 4, 2006, pp. 259–287.

Semitiel-Garcia, Maria, and Pedro Noguera-Mendez, "The Structure of Inter-Industry Systems and the Diffusion of Innovations: The Case of Spain," *Technological Forecasting and Social Change*, Vol. 79, No. 8, 2012, pp. 1548–1567.

Strauss, Anselm, and Juliet Corbin, "Grounded Theory Methodology: An Overview," in Norman K. Denzin and Yvonna S. Lincoln, eds., *The SAGE Handbook of Qualitative Research*, Thousand Oaks, Calif.: SAGE Publications, 1994, pp. 273–285.

Teach for All, *Leadership and Global Learning for Community Impact: 2019 Annual Project Report (July 2018–September 2019)*, New York, 2019, Not available to the general public.

TFA—*See* Teach for All.

UNESCO—*See* United Nations Educational, Scientific and Cultural Organization.

United Nations Educational, Scientific and Cultural Organization, *Education 2030: Incheon Declaration and Framework for Action for the Implementation of Sustainable Development Goal 4*, New York, ED-2016/WS/28, 2016a. As of March 8, 2021: https://unesdoc.unesco.org/ark:/48223/pf0000245656

———, *Girls and Women's Literacy with a Lifelong Learning Perspective: Issues, Trends and Implications for Sustainable Development Goals*, New York, 2016b. As of March 8, 2021: https://unesdoc.unesco.org/ark:/48223/pf0000244959

———, *Global Education Monitoring Report, 2019: Migration, Displacement, and Education; Building Bridges, Not Walls*, New York, 2018. As of March 20, 2021: https://unesdoc.unesco.org/ark:/48223/pf0000265866

———, *Global Education Monitoring Report, 2020: Inclusion and Education; All Means All*, New York, 2020. As of March 8, 2021: https://en.unesco.org/gem-report/report/2020/inclusion

United Nations Educational, Scientific and Cultural Organization, Institute for Statistics, *New Methodology Shows That 258 Million Children, Adolescents and Youth Are Out of School*, New York, UIS/2019/ED/FS/56, 2019. As of March 8, 2021: http://uis.unesco.org/sites/default/files/documents/new-methodology-shows-258-million-children-adolescents-and-youth-are-out-school.pdf

UNW—*See* UN Women.

UN Women, *UN Women Second Change Education Programme: First Annual Report 2018–2019*, New York, 2019, Not available to the general public.

———, *UN Women Second Chance Education and Vocational Learning Programme (SCE): 2020 Annual Report*, New York, 2020, Not available to the general public.

U.S. Agency for International Development, *Glossary of Evaluation Terms*, Washington, D.C., March 25, 2009. As of March 12, 2021: https://pdf.usaid.gov/pdf_docs/PNADO820.pdf

Valente, Thomas W., "Network Models of the Diffusion of Innovations," *Computational and Mathematical Organization Theory*, Vol. 2, No. 2, 1996, pp. 163–164.

———, "Network Interventions," *Science*, Vol. 337, No. 6090, 2012, pp. 49–53.

Valente, Thomas W., Lawrence A. Palinkas, Sara Czaja, Kar-Hai Chu, and C. Hendricks Brown, "Social Network Analysis for Program Implementation," *PLOS One*, Vol. 10, No. 6, 2015.

Wasserman, Stanley, and Katherine Faust, *Social Network Analysis: Methods and Applications*, New York: Cambridge University Press, 1994.

Wimbush, Erica, Steve Montague, and Tamara Mulherin, "Applications of Contribution Analysis to Outcome Planning and Impact Evaluation," *Evaluation*, Vol. 18, No. 3, 2012, pp. 310–329.

Winthrop, Rebecca, Gib Bulloch, Pooja Bhatt, and Arthur Wood, *Investment in Global Education: A Strategic Imperative for Business*, Washington, D.C.: Center for Universal Education at Brookings, Accenture, and Global Business Coalition for Education, 2013. As of March 8, 2021: https://www.brookings.edu/wp-content/uploads/2016/06/Investment-in-Global-Education-Final-web.pdf

World Bank, *What, Why, and How of the Systems Approach for Better Education Results (SABER) (Conference Edition)*, Washington, D.C., April 2013. As of March 8, 2021: http://wbgfiles.worldbank.org/documents/hdn/ed/saber/supporting_doc/Background/SABER_Overview_Paper.pdf

———, *Learning to Realize Education's Promise: World Development Report*, Washington, D.C., 2018a. As of March 8, 2021:
https://www.worldbank.org/en/publication/wdr2018

———, "We Are Living a Learning Crisis," Washington, D.C., October 2018b. As of March 8, 2021:
http://documents1.worldbank.org/curated/en/821801540479977693/pdf/131338-WP-OverviewBalivWEB.pdf

———, *Ending Learning Poverty: What Will It Take?* Washington, D.C., 2019a. As of March 8, 2021:
https://openknowledge.worldbank.org/handle/10986/32553

———, "Global Policy Education Dashboard," brief, January 17, 2019b. As of March 11, 2021:
https://www.worldbank.org/en/topic/education/brief/global-education-policy-dashboard

———, "Education Reforms to Enhance Innovation, Entrepreneurship and Productivity in Georgia," press release, May 29, 2019c. As of March 21, 2021:
https://www.worldbank.org/en/news/press-release/2019/05/29/education-reforms-to-enhance-innovation-entrepreneurship-and-productivity-in-georgia